# DIY GREENHOUSE

The Step By Step Guide To Build A Year-Round Solar Greenhouse And Grow Herbs, Organic Fruits And Vegetables, Plants, And Flowers
[No Prior Experience Required]

# Table of Contents

## How to Use this Book

## Section I: Introduction

1. The Problem - Short Growing Season and Low Overnight Temperatures
2. The Solution - A Simple, Low-Cost Wood and PVC A-Frame Greenhouse

## Section II: Building the 8'x10' Wood & PVC A-Frame Greenhouse

1. Step 1: Site Selection
2. Step 2: List of Building Materials
3. Step 3: Build the Base Frame
4. Step 4: Level and Square the Base Frame
5. Step 5: Build the Upper Frame
6. Step 6: Build the Door Frame
7. Step 7: Build and Attach Roof Section
8. Step 8: Complete Door Frame
9. Step 9: Build the PVC A-Frame Roof
10. Step 10: Save $ - Make Your Own PVC Clamps
11. Step 11: Cover The Greenhouse
12. Step 12: Build and Attach the Door
13. Step 13: Optional Removable Side Panels

## Section III: Results, FAQs, Notes, Info & Resources

1. Results: A Work in Progress
2. Frequently Asked Questions
3. Additional Notes about Using the Greenhouse

4. Additional Information on Measuring, Marking and Cutting Lumber
5. A Note about Using Pressure Treated Wood in Your Garden
6. PVC Pros, Cons, Information and PVC Safety Precautions
7. Notes about Plastic Sheeting
8. Additional Methods for Attaching Plastic Sheeting to the Greenhouse
9. Additional Greenhouse Covering Materials
10. Resources

## Section IV: Lists of Figures and Tables

1. List of Figures
2. List of Tables

### How to Use this Book

This Book begins with an Introduction with two short chapters that explain the problems we have growing vegetables in our cold, high elevation climate and how our simple greenhouses solve the problem.

The plans for the 8'x10' Wood & PVC A-Frame Greenhouse are in Section II.

- Section II is divided into 13 short chapters (see Table of Contents) that correspond to the 13 Major Steps to build the greenhouse.
- Each Major Step (Chapter) begins with the goal and an explanation for that step and lists the smaller steps necessary to complete the major step. Example Steps 3A, 3B and 3C.
- Each of these smaller steps are then explained in detail and when necessary are further broken down into simpler tasks.
- Pictures and/or Diagrams are at the end of each Step.
- Since this book has been designed as an ebook, the Sections, Chapters, Figures and Tables are hot-linked so you can jump anywhere in the book to find what you need. Use the back button on your Kindle to return.

I apologize in advance, because for many of you, this will have too much detail. Many of you will be able to look at the pictures, the diagrams and the cut list and get right to work. I am hoping this will be some people's first DIY construction project so the extra detail could be helpful.

Section III is the reference section that includes

- Results we've had from our greenhouses
- Frequently Asked Questions and Answers
- Additional Notes
- Additional Information relevant to the greenhouse
- Greenhouse related resources

Section IV is a list of 93 Figures and 6 Tables.

**Time Estimate for Building the Greenhouse**

I have estimated the amount of time it will take to complete this project. Some of the "Major Steps" could be completed in 5 minutes (Step 1; Site Selection) and some steps are optional (Step 9; Make Your Own PVC Clamps & Step 13, Optional Removable Side Panels), so you may not do them at all.

Building the Base Frame (Step 3) for example, requires no cuts and only consists of screwing four boards together to form a large box. Many of you can do this in less than 5 minutes, but a first-timer may take 20 or 30 minutes.

Depending upon the slope of your land and how many large rocks have to be moved, leveling the Base Frame (Step 4) may take only a few minutes for some, but will take hours for others. I had to stop everything to rent a hammer drill to break up a boulder that I could not pry out of the way. Except for going to the builder supply store to buy the materials, leveling the frame was the most time consuming step for me.

It may also take some only about 20 minutes to build the PVC A-frame section (Step 9) of the roof while others may take an hour or more.

The time estimates for cutting and attaching the plastic sheeting (Step 11) can also vary tremendously depending upon if it is windy or not and whether or not you have a helper.

For most, this project should be completed in a weekend. I estimate that those experienced with construction will complete this greenhouse in 4 hours. I can imagine many first time DIY projects taking 14 - 16 hours; still "do-able" in a weekend, barring any major problems like I had breaking up and moving a large rock.

**Good Luck**

If you are reading this, I probably don't have to convince you to grow your own vegetables. So Good Luck with building your greenhouse. I hope this book and the greenhouse design will be useful and that you will soon be enjoying fresh home-grown veggies that you grew in your own greenhouse.

# Section I: Introduction

## The Problem - Short Growing Season & Low Overnight Temperatures

We live at about 41° North latitude and at 5,700 ft elevation. The minimum night time temperatures here average 40.9°F in June, 47.1°F in July and 45.8°F in August. Combine that with a late Spring and early Fall frosts, you can see our problem. Needless to say, we live in an area that makes it difficult to grow warm weather vegetables.

Many of our favorite garden vegetables do not grow well until the night time temperatures stay above 60° F and we may have only 20-30 nights with temperatures above 50° F all Summer.

Prior to building our first greenhouse, we had very little success growing tomatoes and egg plant and almost no success trying to grow peppers, cantaloupe, watermelon and okra. In two separate seasons, we harvested only a handful of peppers, but never got a ripe cantaloupe or watermelon.

Our funniest experiment was trying to grow okra without a greenhouse. Okra plants normally grow 6-8 feet tall in warm climates, but the few okra plants that survived were tiny bonsai-like plants barely a foot tall and they produced only a few tiny pods, about the size of a large pea. I wish I had a picture.

After trying to grow warm weather vegetables for several years, it was obvious we needed some kind of "greenhouse" to:

1. Increase the day time soil and air temperatures earlier in the spring
2. Raise the night-time temperatures during the summer
3. Allow the plants to survive late spring and early fall frosts to extend the growing season

We have used the PVC A-Frame Greenhouse described in my other book (_How to Build a Small A-Frame Greenhouse with PVC Pipe and Plastic Sheeting for Less Than $50_) for three growing seasons. The original 5x10 green house solved our problem of trying to grow peppers. The simple PVC A-Frame fits over our garden beds, is easy to set up and to take down and store, and is easy to move from one bed to another.

Since we started using a greenhouse, we have had bountiful pepper harvests every year, and by using a temporary PVC frame and plastic sheeting, we have been able to harvest more ripe tomatoes as well. But it was time for us to build a larger greenhouse to increase our tomato harvest and to try grow a few more of our favorite vegetables.

If you have spent any time at all pricing greenhouses, you already know that buying a greenhouse kit can cost thousands of dollars or you can spend $400 or $500 on a flimsy piece of plastic with a zipper that someone proudly calls a cold frame. Partly because of budget, but mostly because of pride, I just can't allow myself to spend that much money on a kit. This was going to have to be another DIY project.

## The Solution - A Simple, Low-Cost Wood and PVC A-Frame Greenhouse

I call this project a Wood and PVC A-Frame greenhouse. My previous "greenhouse" could be described as a Low Tunnel or Hoop House, but shaped as an A-Frame instead of a hoop. This project is basically the same A-Frame design, except it is elevated off the ground so it is tall enough to walk into. Since the greenhouse has a door, it requires a door frame, which is made from wood. The Door side of the greenhouse looks like a gable-type greenhouse and the opposite end looks like an 8-foot high Hoop House.

Currently, I still cover my greenhouse with utility grade 6 mil plastic sheeting, but the wooden parts of the greenhouse frame could be covered with glass or other rigid materials (see [Additional Greenhouse Covering Materials](#)).

## Types of Greenhouses & Greenhouse Terminology

There are several types of Greenhouses and much of the terminology seems to be interchangeable. A Hoop House or Low Tunnel sold or described at one place looks a lot like a Cold Frame sold at another place.

- **Row Cover** - is a very low, covered tunnel made from metal or plastic hoops that support a plastic cover. A row cover is only high enough to cover the plants in one or two rows. Except for an irrigation system, row covers, would usually not include any additional technology.
- **Cold Frame, Low Tunnel or Hoop House** - are apparently different names to describe a design that is similar to a row cover, except that the hoops span a larger height and width. Low Cold Frames, tunnels or hoop houses also would not include much technology except for irrigation.
- **High Tunnel** - refers to a design similar to a Low Tunnel, except the walls are built higher to provide more height inside for moving equipment and for better air circulation. High Tunnels usually begin to incorporate more technology into the system.
- **Greenhouse** - What we typically think of as a greenhouse is usually a rectangular shaped house (Gable) with glass or other rigid panels on the walls and the roof. A true greenhouse is tall enough to move around easily and allow for good air circulation. Many greenhouses today, usually include a high degree of automated technology. Greenhouses can also be skillion shaped design (Roof high on one end to allow sunshine or to provide ventilation). A row of connected skillion greenhouses are referred to as a

Saw-tooth greenhouse design.

## Greenhouse Building Materials

For the DIY guy building a greenhouse, the most common building materials would be wood, rebar or PVC pipe. Other materials require welding or special pipe bending tools. I decided on PVC pipe, because I wanted to be able to move our first greenhouse from one raised bed to another between seasons. I concluded that it would be much easier to move PVC pipe than a wooden frame that was nailed or bolted together or a rebar frame that was "tied" together, especially if I temporarily attached the PVC pipe.

The PVC frame structure worked so well, I continue to use it for this new Wood and PVC A-Frame greenhouse project. I use untreated lumber for this project, but modern treated lumber would be safe. See additional information in Section V (Our Results, FAQs, Notes & Resources) about:

- Using Pressure Treated Wood in Your Garden
- PVC Pros - Cons & Info And PVC Safety Precautions

## The Wood & PVC A-frame Greenhouse

The finished Wood and PVC A-Frame greenhouse (8 feet wide; 10 feet long) can be seen in Figure 1, Fig. 2, Fig. 3, & Fig. 4 show . The door is 72 inches high and 28 inches wide.

Ventilation can be controlled by opening the door and vents at each end. I also added removable panels (optional) that increased ventilation and allowed easier access to the plants (for us and for bees).

**Figure 1.** The Wood and PVC A-Frame Greenhouse Early in the 2012 growing season. Notice door and two access panels are open for ventilation.

**Figure 2.** The Wood and PVC A-Frame Greenhouse late 2012 Growing Season.

**Figure 3.** Our Raised Beds and Both Greenhouses Late in the 2012 Growing Season.

Figure 4. Front View of Greenhouses late 2012 Growing Season.

# Section II: Building the 8x10 foot Wood & PVC A-Frame Greenhouse

This section provides plans the 8x10 foot Wood & PVC A-Frame Greenhouse that we built.

**Major Steps to Building the 8x10 foot Wood & PVC A-Frame Greenhouse:**

1. Site Selection
2. List of Building Materials
3. Build the Base Frame
4. Level and Square the Base Frame
5. Build the Upper Frame
6. Build the Door Frame
7. Build and Attach Roof Section
8. Complete Door Frame
9. Build the PVC A-Frame Roof
10. Save $ & Make Your Own PVC Clamps
11. Cover the Greenhouse
12. Build and Attach the Door
13. Option: Build Removable Side Panels

**Step 1: Site Selection**

Before we start building, we need to decide where and how big the greenhouse is going to be. We were running out of places in our yard to add more raised beds or greenhouses. Because space is limited and also because I didn't want to spend a lot of money on an unproven greenhouse design, the greenhouse had to be relatively small.

In Figure 5, you can see we had just enough space to build a greenhouse that was about 8 feet wide. There was enough room, that we could have built the greenhouse as long as 12-15 feet, but the land slopes off very steeply to the right side of the photo. The drop off was so steep, I considered shortening the greenhouse to avoid the slope, but decided the slope could be built up and chose a final length of 10 feet.

**Figure 5.** Our Raised Garden Beds Showing the Future Site of the New Greenhouse. This was in early spring of 2012, the A-frame greenhouse had been assembled and peas were coming up in another raised bed.

I wanted to build a greenhouse very similar to the PVC A-Frame in Figure 5, but needed a greenhouse that was taller. The short A-frames work very well for peppers and egg plant, but are not really tall enough for tomatoes or okra.

The plan as I first envisioned it, was simply an elevated wooden frame with another PVC A-Frame greenhouse on top of it. I decided this would work, but it would be a lot nicer to actually have a door to walk through instead of a plastic flap. So the final plan is a 48 inch wooden frame with a 72 inch door on one end with a PVC A-frame structure for the roof (Figure 1, Fig. 2, Fig. 3, & Fig. 4).

**Steps for choosing the Building Site:**
Step 1A: Measure the Slope
Step 1B: Decide on Greenhouse Orientation
Step 1C: Decide on Size of Greenhouse
Step 1D: Determine if Site has Acceptable Clearance

**Step 1A: Measure the Slope**
The slope of your building site is very important. If the site is flat or if it slopes very little, you can build a structure any size as long as you have room. If the slope is very steep, you will be limited to building small structures unless you move lots of dirt or build a split level greenhouse.

To measure slope over a short distance, you can use a carpenters level and a straight 10 foot board or a simple string or line level. If the rise or drop is less than 11.25 inches in 10 feet, the slope if flat enough to build the greenhouse with 2x12 Lumber for the base frame. The base frame for the greenhouse is basically a raised bed.

I suggest you use 2x12 lumber for the base frame because it is heavy and will work for a larger variety of slopes. If you have a very flat building site, you could use smaller lumber such as 2x8 or 2x10 but may need to attach the frame to stakes or concrete blocks so the base frame can act as a good foundation for the greenhouse.

If the rise or drop of your site is only 8 inches over a 10 foot length, 2 x 10 boards would be wide enough for the base frame and if the rise or drop of your site is only 6 inches over the 10 foot length, 2 x 8 boards would be wide enough to create a base frame.

If the rise or drop is greater than the width of a 2 x 12 (11.25 inches), you will have to move some dirt, or build a shorter greenhouse (See Figure 6, Fig. 7, Fig. 8, Fig. 9 & Fig. 10 below).

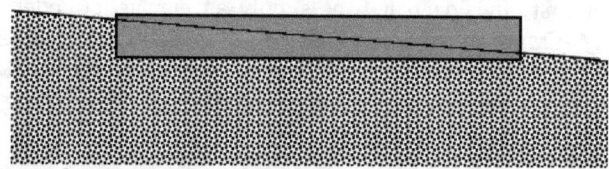

**Figure 6.** Example of a Site with a Mild Slope. The slope is not more than the depth of the base frame over the 10 foot length. This site is suitable to build a 10 foot long base frame with minimal effort.

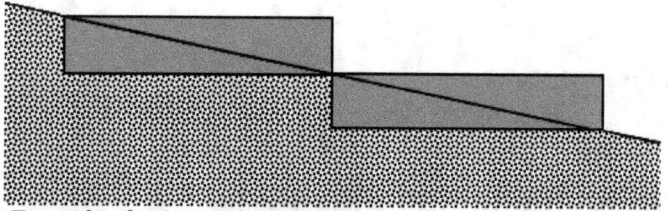

**Figure 7.** Example of a Site with a Steep Slope. The slope is twice the depth of the base frame over the 10 foot length. In this example, the greenhouse base frame can only be 5 feet long unless the base is built like stair steps. Another option is to excavated up slope and add soil down slope as shown in Figure 8.

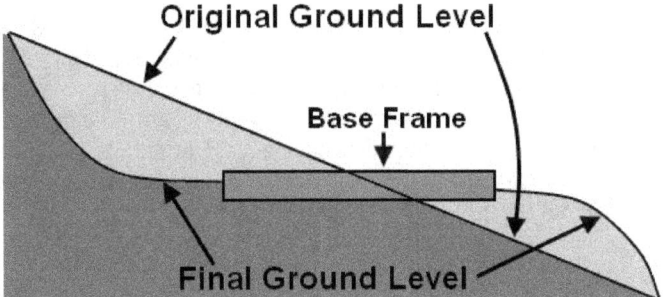

**Figure 8.** Example of Site with Steep Slope. Soil has to be excavated from up slope and deposited down slope to create a level site for the base frame.

My building site was moderately sloped, but had a severe drop off on the downhill side. Figure 9 shows a diagram of the base frame in relation to the slope. You can see the down hill side needs to be supported. Figure 10 shows how the downhill side was supported with large stones. I also drove stakes into the ground which were screwed into the base frame. I used landscape fabric to prevent soil from washing out between the stones. I originally planned to mix a few bags of concrete to pour in among the stones, but they are well set into the soil and are extremely sturdy, so I have not yet used the concrete.

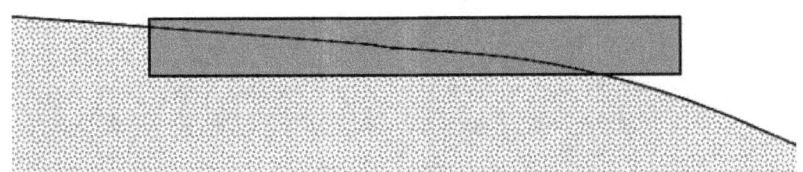

**Figure 9.** Example of Slope at My Building Site.

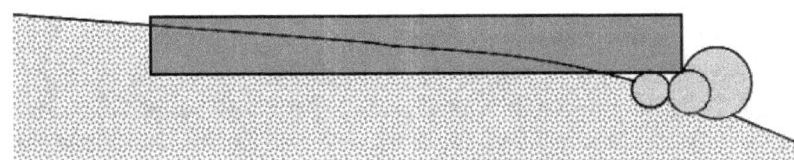

**Figure 10.** Example of Slope at My Building Site. I used large stones to support the downhill end of the base frame. Additional large stones were stacked against that end of the greenhouse for additional support.

**Step 1B: Decide on Greenhouse Orientation**

In a perfect world, your building site will allow the greenhouse to orient the length along an East-West Line, so the best Sun exposure will hit the South side of the greenhouse with minimal lose of sunlight (North side for Southern Hemisphere).

The greenhouse will work oriented in any direction, but an an East-West orientation will cast the least shadows on the plants. A North-South greenhouse will shade itself the most.

If you plan to use a building space next to an existing structure that is oriented Northeast - Southwest, it may not look right to build a greenhouse with a different orientation, but you will have to decide which is most important to you, looks of function.

**Step 1C: Decide on Size of Greenhouse**

Most sites will be suitable for building a small 8x10 foot greenhouse like the design in this book. It would be a simple task to keep the 8 foot width and extend the greenhouse 12, 14, 16 or 20 feet long. This part of FAQ Section discusses expanding the Greenhouse to lengths of 12-20 feet and Table 6 shows the materials needed for those increased lengths.

**Step 1D: Determine if Site has Acceptable Clearance**

Sometimes before building on a new site, it looks like there is plenty of clearance, then later you find out it hard to squeeze between the building and the fence. If you want a lawn mower or wheel barrow to fit between the greenhouse and a fence or another building, make sure now before you start construction. Also, the greenhouse has a door and it will need at least two more inches than the door width for the door to swing open.

It is also important to make sure other buildings or trees don't cast shadows on the greenhouse. If this is not possible, choose a site that allows the most sunlight. If you have a choice, choose morning sunlight over afternoon sunlight, since warming the greenhouse early in the day is very important.

**Step 2: List of Building Materials** Table 1 below is the list of building materials for the 8 x 10 foot hybrid wood and PVC Greenhouse. I included the price I paid for most items. I bought all the lumber and hardware in Spring of 2012 and the PVC pipe in Spring 2010.

Based on the number of cuts needed for the greenhouse, there are three different lengths of 2x4s in the materials lists. This makes it slightly more complicated to buy materials, but it reduces cost and waste. The 2x4 precut studs are 92 5/8 inches and usually cost less than a full sized 8 foot 2x4. It is also less expensive to buy a single 10 ft board instead of two studs for cutting three, 34 or 36 inch cross braces for a 34 or 36 inch door.

**Table 1. Materials List and My Cost for the 8 x 10 foot Wood & PVC A-Frame Green House.**

| N | Material List 8 X 10 Foot Greenhouse | My Cost |
|---|---|---|
| 2 | 2 x 12 x 10 feet Un-treated Lumber | $23.20 |
| 2 | 2 x 12 x 8 feet Un-treated Lumber | $18.56 |
| 9 | 2 x 4 x 10 feet Un-treated Lumber | $34.20 |
| 2 | 2 x 4 x 8 feet Un-treated Lumber | $6.08 |
| 6 | 2 x 4 x 92 5/8 Un-treated Stud | $13.62 |
| 17 | 1 x 2 x 8 feet Furring Strips | $19.04 |
| 11 | 3/4 inch PVC pipe 10 feet | $13.75 |
| 10 | 1 inch EMT Conduit Straps 2-hole metal | $4.05 |
| 1 lb | #10 3.5 inch Exterior Screws | $8.47 |
| 1 lb | #10 3 inch Exterior Screws | $8.47 |
| 1 lb | #10 3 inch Exterior Screws | $5.99 |
| 1 lb | #10 1.5 inch Exterior Screws | $5.50 |
| 1 | 100 pack #8 flat washer (zinc) | $4.24 |
| 2 | 2.5 inch zinc hinges | $5.95 |
| 2 | Rolls 6 mil Plastic Sheeting (10x25 feet) | $49.96 |
| 1 | Pack 8 inch UV cable ties | $5.99 |
| 16 | PVC Clamps (home made) | $0.00 |
| | Tax | $14.44 |
| | **Total Cost** | **$241.51** |

## Step 3: Build the Base Frame

Much of the strength of the greenhouse comes from the Base Frame, which acts as a foundation. The base frame is basically a raised garden bed frame built from 2x12 lumber. Due to the weight of the lumber and the fact the frame is partially to mostly buried, the frame is very heavy and is extremely stable.

Of course a concrete foundation will be stronger and last longer, but that also adds construction time, costs and complexity to the project. I have untreated raised beds that are still strong after five years. I expect our untreated base frame to last at least 10 years in my cold climate. An untreated frame may not last that long in your climate, but treated lumber would last at least 10 years (see Note about Using Pressure Treated Wood in Your Garden).

**Steps to Build the Base Frame**
Step 3A: Use the Correct Base Frame Layout
Step 3B: Mark and Drill Pilot Holes in Base Frame Ends
Step 3C: Screw Frame Together
Optional Step: Attach Angles or Corner Brackets for Additional Strength

**Step 3A: Use the Correct Base Frame Layout**
There are three basic ways to assemble both the base and elevated frames (Figure 11).
**The plans in this book use example "A"** which provides minimum width and maximize length. The 10 foot 2x12 lumber fits inside of the 8 foot 2x12 lumber. If you use examples B or C, you will have to adjust some of the measurements (such as roof length or angle) so they will fit correctly. None of the 2x12 lumber used for the Base Frames needs to be cut (See Cut List; Table 2). To visualize what the base frame should look like, refer back to Figure 5 or look ahead to Figure 20 & Fig. 21.

**Step 3B: Mark and Drill Pilot Holes in Base Frame Ends**
Most lumber framing is simply done with hammer and nails, but if holes are pre-drilled and screws are used instead, the frame will fit tighter, last longer, warp less and the boards will not split as easily.

- Start by marking the width of a 2x4 on each end that is to be drilled (Fig.

12), then evenly space 3 marks near the center of the marked area, so you can drill holes that will penetrate near the center of the end board.
- Make sure to use exterior screws that are long enough to hold the boards together for many years. The screw shown in Figure 13, is #10 screw that is 3.5 inches long.
- Use a drill bit that is slightly narrower than the screws you plan to use. A 1/8th inch drill bit is recommended for #10 screws in softwood. For a 3.5 inch screw, the bit should be about 3 inches long.
- Drill the pilot hole through both the face of one board and through the end of the other board (Fig. 14).

**Step 3C: Screw Frame Together**

- After drilling the pilot holes, start the screws and let them extend about quarter inch out of each hole on the other side of the board so you will be able to feel when the screws fit into the holes on the other board (Fig. 15). This will help line the boards up and hold them in their proper place. For the 12 inch base frame boards, I used three screws per corner. You could use four screws if you like, but three will be very strong.
- After you are sure the extended tip of the screw is in the pre-drilled hole on the other board, line both boards as straight as possible and hold as firmly as possible and drive the screw all the way in (Fig. 16).

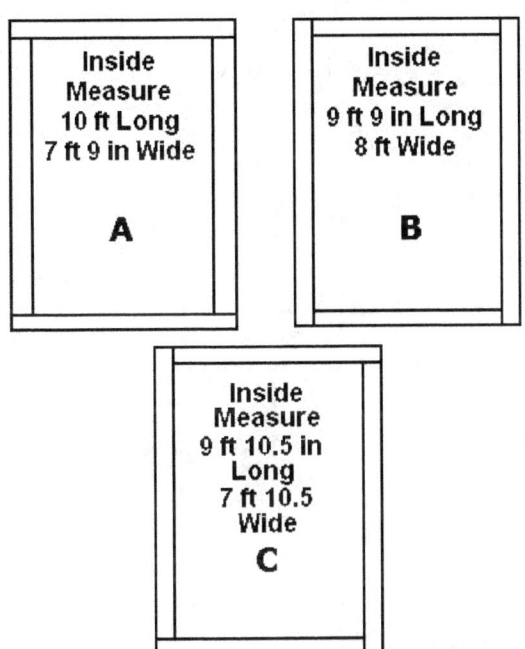

**Figure 11.** Three Different Ways to Connect an 8 x 10 ft Frame. This Plan uses Example A for the Base Frame.

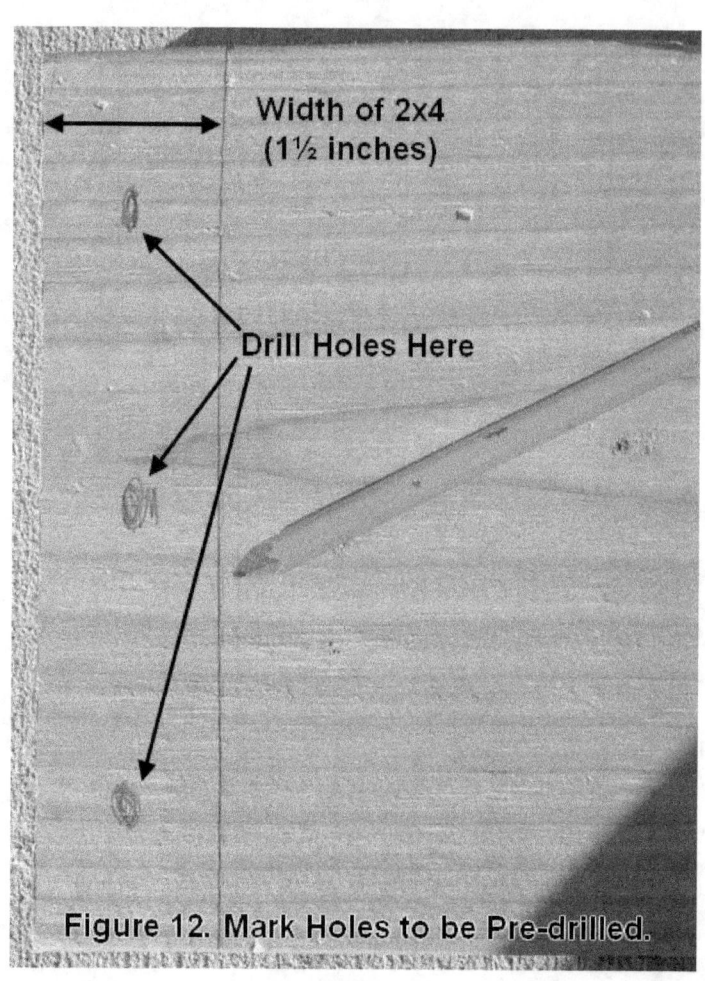
Figure 12. Mark Holes to be Pre-drilled.

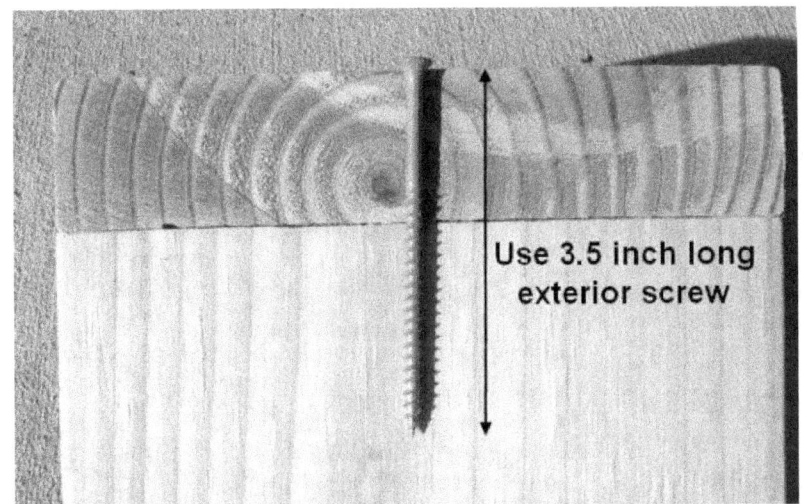

**Figure 13.** Use Long Screws for a Strong Frame. This is a #10 exterior screw, 3.5 inches long.

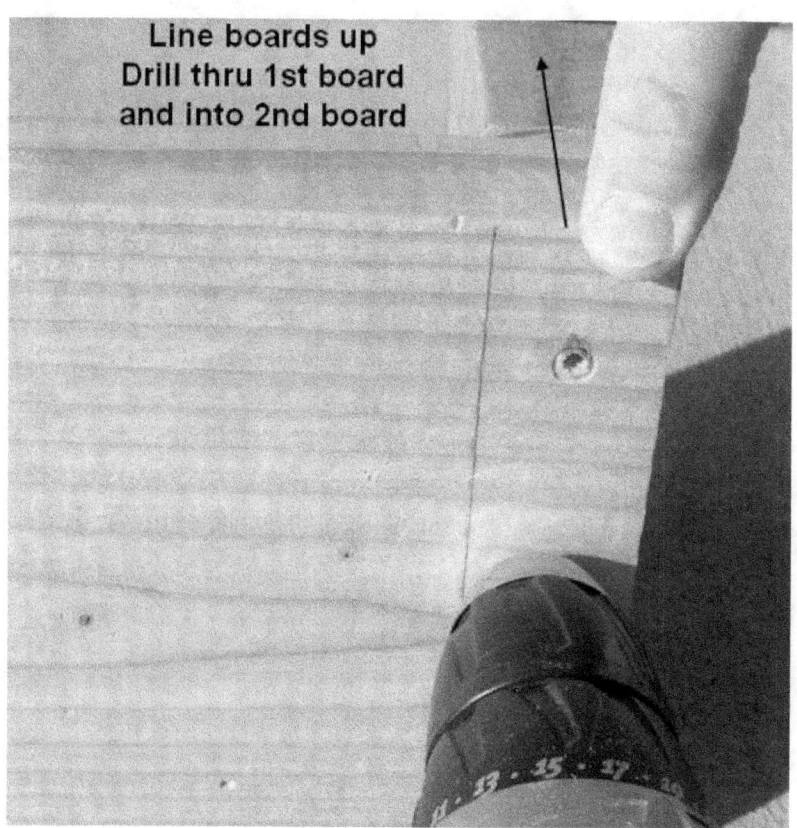

**Figure 14.** Drill Pilot Holes. In this case drill through both the face of one board & through the end of the other board.

**Figure 15.** Start Screws. Let them extend about quarter inch so you can feel them fit into the holes on the other board.

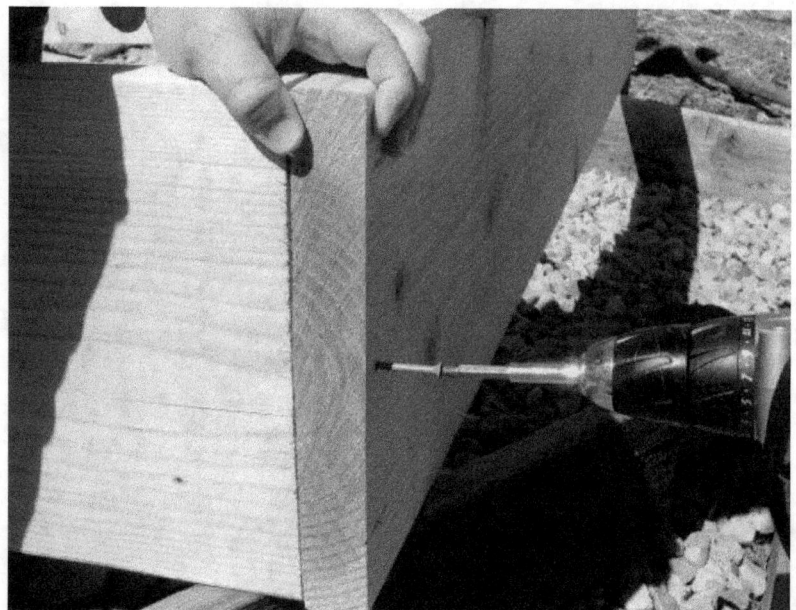

**Figure 16.** Hold Frame Firmly while Driving Screws. The example in the photo has only one screws started. Sometimes it is faster to start all 3 screws at once, line them up in the 3 holes and then screw them all the way down, one at a time.

**Optional Step: Attach Angles or Corner Brackets for Additional Strength**

There are many types of angles and corner brackets ranging from about 50 cents to $15 that will add strength to the corners. Some are so strong, they would hold the base frame together without additional screws, but they are expensive and require bolts to hold the angles to the frame.

If you built the frame properly, with good exterior screws, the frame will last for many years without additional support.

## Step 4: Level and Square the Base Frame

As with any construction project, it is important that the foundation be level and square. This project is no different. If the Base Frame is not level and square, the lumber cuts will not fit together properly. If you take a little extra time and care to make sure the frame is level and square, the project will be simpler in the long run.

### Steps to Level and Square the Base Frame

Step 4A: Place Frame Close to the Final Location
Step 4B: Square the Base Frame
Step 4C: Use Level to Determine High and Low Areas
Step 4D: Dig High Areas Down and Fill Low Areas
Step 4E: Final Check Frame for Square and Level
Step 4F: Back-fill around Base Frame with Soil or Gravel

### Step 4A: Place Frame Close to the Final Location

Figure 17, shows my finished base frame moved into position to be squared, leveled and then partially buried into the ground. This will be your last chance to make sure the frame is properly spaced from other structures. I had covered the area with landscape fabric and gravel. Before I could start leveling and squaring the frame, I had to rake the gravel out of the way and move all the tomato stakes.

### Step 4B: Square the Base Frame

I am covering squaring the frame first, but both leveling and squaring have to go together. You can have the frame perfectly level, but be out of square and vice versa. Any adjustment to one effects the other. Depending upon how much of a perfectionist you are determines how close to square and level you make your frame.

If the frame is square, it helps everything fit together properly, but it doesn't have to be perfect. This is rough framing not fine cabinetry work. The best way to square the frame is to make sure the measurement across the outside diagonals are the same. For example, the outside diagonal measurements (Fig. 18) should be just a hair over 156 inches long. If they are within a quarter of an inch, bump it one time and measure again. That's probably close enough for a garden frame.

### Step 4C: Use a Level to Determine High and Low Areas

To level the frame, use a carpenters level. Even if you have a perfectly level site, you still need to dig a trench so the base frame sits down into the ground at least 3 inches to increase the base's strength. Six to eight inches would be better. Keep in mind, the lower into the ground the Base Frame sits, the lower the door's threshold. For a sloping site, you will dig down on the uphill side until it is level with the low side.

**Refer back to the Site Selection Chapter:**

- Figure 6
- Figure 7
- Figure 8
- Figure 9
- Figure 10

### Step 4D: Dig High Areas Down and Fill Low Areas

To remove the soil from the high areas, you will have to prop up the Base Frame with a board, rock or concrete block until there is room for a shovel, pry bar or pick axe. After all the high places are identified and dug out, check the level again. Then identify and remove the new high spots. Repeat the process until the frame is level. This is a back and forth process as the frame "see-saws" it's way down into the ground.

Then, when satisfied the frame is deep enough into the ground and is level, fill any low areas with soil or gravel and tamp it with a board or pry bar.

Figure 19 & Figure 20 show various stages of the leveling process and Figure 21 shows the final position of the base frame. Notice in Figure 22, the large rock on top of the frame to hold the frame in position. The frame had not yet been back-filled with soil.

### Step 4E: Final Check Frame for Square and Level

Make sure the base frame is still level on all 4 sides and across all 4 corners and keep checking the diagonal measurements to keep the frame square.

### Step 4F: Back-fill around Base Frame with Soil or Gravel

We need to fill all areas around the base frame with soil or gravel to help hold it in place. But before we do this, we want to consider the Vertical Supports that need to be attached on the outside of the base frame.

If the frame is not solid, tamp the soil down around the base frame and check again. If it is still not sturdy, drive several stakes into the ground next to the frame and screw the stakes into the base frame.

**Figure 17.** Finished Base Frame. The frame has been placed close to where I intend to build the greenhouse.

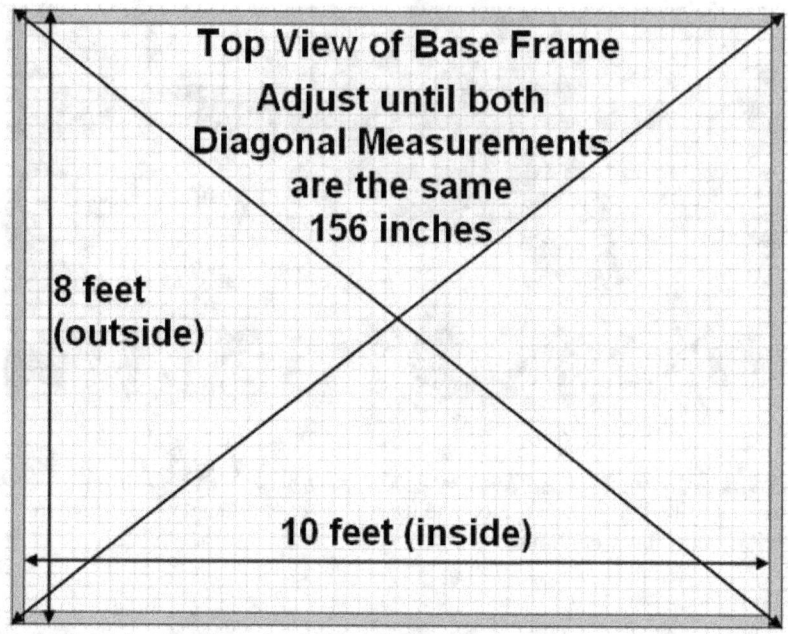

**Figure 18.** Scale Drawing of 8 ft X 10 ft Bed Frame. The actual outside measure is 10 ft 3 inches x 8 feet and the actual inside measure is 10 ft x 7 feet 9 inches. The diagram shows where to measure diagonals to square the frame.

**Figure 19.** Leveling the Base Frame I. Notice rock holding frame up so I could remove soil. I used rebar to hold back the landscape fabric and soil and to hold the frame in place during leveling.

**Figure 20.** Leveling the Base Frame II. Almost there.

**Figure 21.** The Base Frame is Level. Measure one more time to make sure frame is also square. Notice the large rock holding frame in position on the front (left side). I waited to back-fill with soil until the Vertical Supports were attached to the frame.

**Figure 22.** Large Rocks Used to Support the Hanging End of My Base Frame. Additional rocks were added to provide weight and support on the downhill side. Stakes were also driven into the ground and screwed into the base frame for additional Support. Landscape fabric was used to hold the soil inside the frame so it won't wash out between the large rocks. I intend to mix and pour a couple of bags of concrete on the large rocks to help hold, but so far it has not been necessary.

## Step 5: Build the Upper Frame

The Upper Frame is basically a 2x4 copy of the 2x12 Base Frame. It is held 48 inches above the Base Frame with 9 Vertical Supports and the Door Frame. The Upper Frame will hold the PVC pipe that makes up the A-Frame.

The 4 Vertical Supports placed in the corners must be marked correctly so their tops are level. The 4 corner Vertical Supports are attached first, then the Upper Frame is constructed. After the Upper Frame is complete, the remaining 5 Vertical Supports are attached. Building the Door Frame is covered in the next chapter.

### Steps to Build the Upper Frame
Step 5A: Mark and Cut Lumber
Step 5B: Mark Framing Layout on Base Frame
Step 5C: Mark and Pre-drill Holes in Vertical Supports
Step 5D: Make 48 inch Mark on 4 Corner Vertical Supports
Step 5E: Attach 4 Vertical Supports to Base Frame Corners
Step 5F: Attach Two Upper Frame End Pieces to Vertical Supports
Step 5G: Attach Two Upper Frame Side Pieces to Upper Frame End Pieces and to Vertical Supports
Step 5H: Attach Remaining Vertical Supports

### Step 5A: Mark and Cut Lumber.
The first step is to cut all of the boards to the desired lengths for the frame (see the cut list in Table 2). Since the 2x12s for the Base Frame do not need to be cut, you could assemble the frame before making any cuts.

In Table 2, the Number (N) and type of Lumber to be cut is shown. The Cut (in) is the length in inches each piece needs to be cut. The Application shows where the pieces will be used and how many you need to cut. All cuts in Table 2 are described here:

### Description of Cuts in Table 2:

1. None of the 10 foot 2x12 lumber (Base Frame Length) needs to be cut.
2. None of the 8 foot 2x12 lumber (Base Frame Width) needs to be cut.
3. Two of the 10 foot 2x4s for the upper frame length also do not need to be

cut.
4. The first pieces to cut are two 10 foot 2x4s cut to 99 inches each are used for the two Upper Frame Widths
5. Five 10 foot 2x4s are cut in half (60 inches), then 9 of these pieces are cut to 59¼ inches for the Vertical Frame Supports. The remaining piece is cut to 48 inches for the Door Frame Top.
6. Two of the 8 foot 2x4s are cut to a 45° angle without cutting any length. These pieces form the roof section and will be trimmed to fit after they are attached.
7. Scrap pieces from the roof section are cut two 24 inch pieces, to fill both Upper Door Frame Sides. For a very tight fit, cut these pieces a wee bit long (1/32) and sand or file them down to fit.
8. One 2x4 stud is cut twice to 44½ inches for the two Lower Door Frame Side Fill pieces. Also cut these pieces a bit long and sand or file them to fit.
9. Two 2x4 studs are cut to 86¾ inches for the two Door Frame Sides.
10. Two 2x4 studs are cut to 71 7/8 inches for the two Door Sides (just under 72 inches so door does not stick).
11. The Top of the Door Frame is cut to 44 inches and is cut from a 60 inch scrap left from cutting the Vertical Supports
12. One 2x4 stud is cut into three pieces (24-30 inches) for Cross Braces. See Table 4 for door widths.

You will notice the cut length for the Door Cross Braces are listed as "24-30". These cuts depend on the size of the door you choose. Table 3 shows additional cuts for 32 - 36 inch wide doors, but these widths require longer lumber as shown in Table 3. Also notice that both Roof Angles should cut to 45° without cutting any length. The two 45° come together to form the roof peak. These boards will be trimmed to fit after installation.

If you don't have much experience measuring, marking or cutting lumber see Additional Information on Measuring, Marking and Cutting Lumber.

**Table 2. Cuts for Lumber to Build the 8x10 Greenhouse.**

| N | Lumber | Cut (in) | Application |
|---|---|---|---|
| 2 | 2 x 12 x 10 feet | uncut | 2 Base Frame Lengths |
| 2 | 2 x 12 x 8 feet | uncut | 2 Base Frame Widths |
| 2 | 2 x 4 x 10 feet | uncut | 2 Upper Frame Lengths |
| 2 | 2 x 4 x 10 feet | 99 | 2 Upper Frame Widths |
| 5 | 2 x 4 x 10 feet | 59 1/4 | 9 vertical supports |
| 2 | 2 x 4 x 8 feet | 45° - trim | 2 Front Roof Angles |
| 1 | 2 x 4 x 93 stud | 44 1/2 | 2 Side Fill lower |
| 2 | scrap from roof | 24 | 2 Side Fill upper |
| 2 | 2 x 4 x 93 stud | 86 3/4 | 2 Door Frame Sides |
| 2 | 2 x 4 x 93 stud | 71 7/8 | 2 Door Sides |
| 1 | vertical scrap | 44 | 1 Door Frame Top |
| 1 | 2 x 4 x 93 stud | 24-30* | 3 Door Cross Braces |

* Cuts are made 1/8 inch short of door frame width.

### Step 5B: Mark Framing Layout on the Base Frame

Figure 23 shows the layout to be marked on the Base Frame. The Diagram is a top-down view with the door on the left. The layout marks are used to line up the Vertical Frame Supports and the Door Frame at the proper places on the Base Frame. The Vertical Frame Supports are shown in black. The Vertical Door Framing pieces are dark gray and the layout shown is for a 28 inch door. The Base Fame is light gray.

If the layout plan in Figure 23 is not perfectly clear, take a few minutes and look at these additional figures:

- Figure 24 (Picture of completed frame)
- Figure 25 (Diagram - Frame front view)
- Figure 26 (Diagram - Frame side view)

**Step 5B Mark Framing Layout on the Base Frame is broken down into 4 tasks:**

- **1: Mark Layout for the Corner Vertical Supports** - Measure 3½ inches from the end of each side or line a 2x4 block (wide direction) up with the edge of the side where it is joined to the end piece and make a mark at the end of the block. The Corners do not cover the end pieces.
- **2: Mark Layout for the Center Vertical Supports on each Side** - Measure 35 1/3 inches from the inside of the corner mark on each end. Mark the width of a 2x4 with a block or measure 3½ inches. The gap between these marks should also be 35 1/3 inches.
- **3: Mark Layout for the Center Vertical Support on the Back** - Measure 46¼ inches from each end and mark. There should be a 3½ inch gap for a single Vertical Support. Our greenhouse has only one support in the back. **If you want two supports instead of one**, mark 29 1/3 inches from each end. Mark 3½ inches (width of 2x4) from each of those marks and it should be another 29 1/3 inches between them.
- **4: Decide on Door Width and Mark Layout for the Door Frame onto the Base Frame** - Measure 48 inches from one end to mark the Center. You can double check by marking 48 inches from the other end. They should match. Measure half the distance of your door on each side of the center mark. If your door is to be 28 inches wide, mark 14 inches on each side of the door. If your door is to be 32 inches wide, mark 16 inches on each side of the door and so on.

**Note about Size of Door and Door Frame**

I chose to build a door 28 inches wide and 72 inches tall. The smaller the door, the less stress on the hinges and the door frame and the less effect the wind has on the door. A 28 inch door might seem narrow, but it is the same width as some of the doors in my house. It allows easy access to the greenhouse with buckets and tools.

If you want the door to be wide enough for a wheel barrow or cart, you may need to build a wider door, but you will also need to make sure the base frame is lower into the ground and/ or build a ramp to get over the threshold.

I added removable panels (see Optional Removable Panels) on one side of the greenhouse to provide additional cooling and to improve access. These openings are wide enough for a wheel barrows and carts until the plants grow and fill the space.

The door can be any width between 24 and 36 inches and I have provided plans and materials for those sizes. For simplicity, all doors are 72 inches high. Just remember you will need additional lumber as shown in Table 3 if the door is more than 30 inches wide.

**Note:** To be perfectly spaced, the Vertical Supports are spaced 35 1/3 inches between each other. But the 1/3 inch is hard to measure. You can think of the 1/3 inch as a "fat" 5/16th (or 5/16th plus a third of a 16th). It really doesn't matter if you do not plan to build the optional removable panels. If you plan on building the panels, if the spaces between the Vertical Supports are not the same, then your panels will be different and may not be interchangeable.

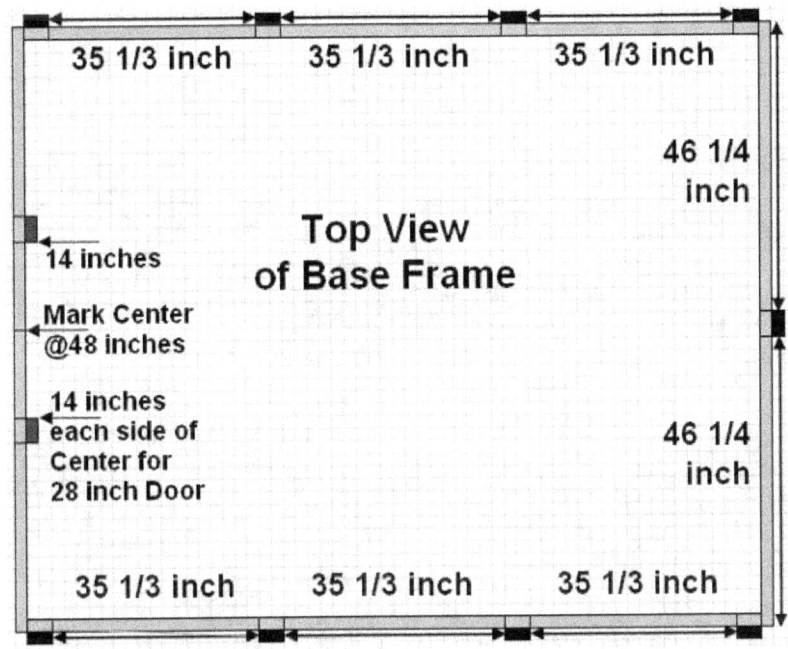

**Figure 23.** Base Frame Layout. Shows Layout Markings for Vertical Supports and for a 28 inch Door.

**Figure 24.** Nearly Completed Wood and PVC A-Frame Greenhouse.

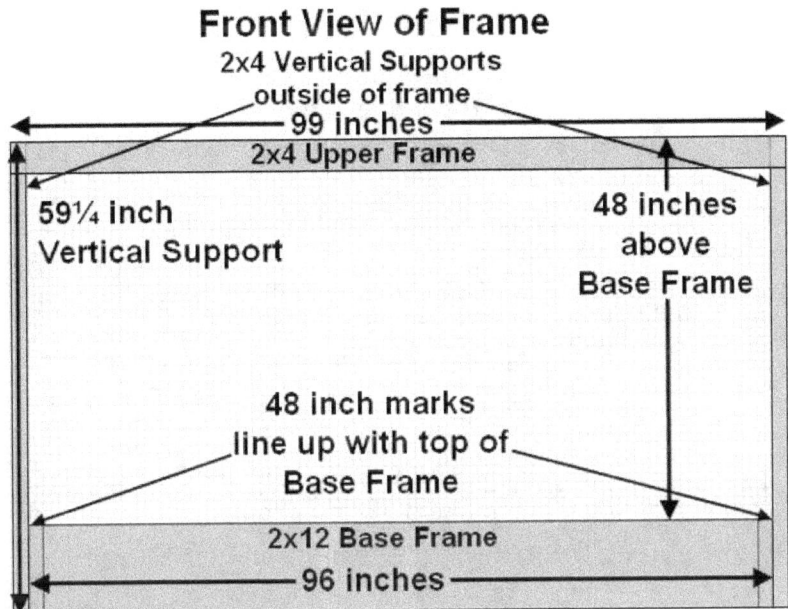

**Figure 25.** Front View of Greenhouse Frame.

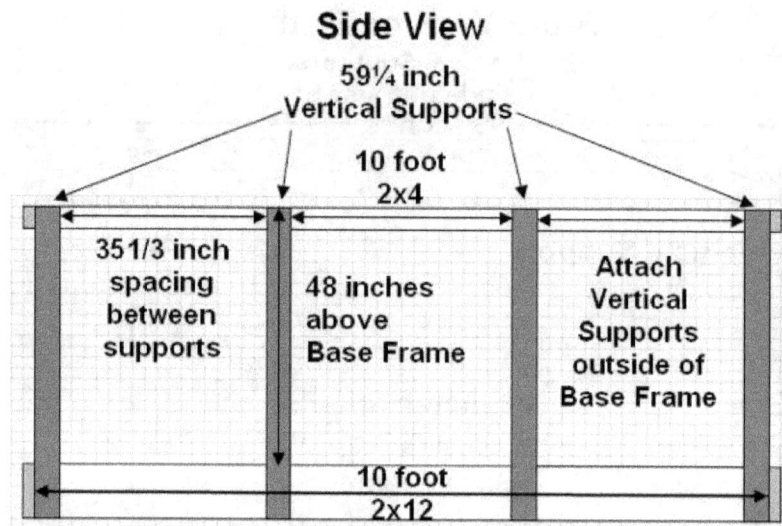

**Figure 26.** Side View of Greenhouse Frame.

**Step 5C: Mark and Pre-drill Holes in Vertical Supports** There are nine Vertical Supports that are all the same length. Four of these will be used in the corners, two on each side and one in the center back. The Corner Vertical Supports are marked, pre-drilled and attached differently than the other five Vertical Supports.

- All 9 Vertical Supports are marked, pre-drilled and attached to the Base Frame the same way.
- The 4 Corner Vertical Supports are marked, pre-drilled and attached to the Upper Frame differently than the 5 Vertical Supports used on the sides and the end.
- Marks measured at 48 inches on the 4 Corner Vertical Supports will make sure the height of the Upper Frame is correct. These marks are not necessary on the remaining 5 Vertical Supports.

**Marking and Pre-drilling Holes in Vertical Supports (Step 5C), requires 4 tasks:**

- **Mark and Pre-drill 5 holes at Bottom of all 9 Vertical Supports** - as shown in the diagram in Fig. 27 and the photo (Fig. 28). Stagger the holes from top to bottom. Don't drill too close to the bottom or too close to the 48 inch line (which will match the top of the Base Frame). I hope you have good quality lumber with few splits, but if there are splits in the wood, move the holes so they do not line up along a split. It would help to put some glue in a split if it is starting to separate. It is not necessary to pre-drill into the sides of the 2x12 they will be attached to.
- **Mark and Pre-drill Holes at Top of the 4 Corner Vertical Supports** - If the tops of the 4 corner Vertical Supports are consistently marked and pre-drilled at ¾ inch and 2¾ from the top of each Vertical Support, we can make sure these screws will not hit the screws that connect from the upper frame later (see Fig. 29).
- **Mark the 4 Vertical Supports** - that are to be used in the corners (same Vertical Supports that have the 48 inch lines) as shown in Fig. 31 at ¾ inch and 2¾ from the top.
- **Mark and Pre-drill Holes at Top of the remaining 5 Vertical Supports** - The placement of screws in the top of these Vertical Supports are not critical as there are no other screws that could interfere. Drill holes for 4 screws anywhere between ¾ and 3¼ inches from the top and at least ¾ inch

from the edge of the board (Fig. 30).

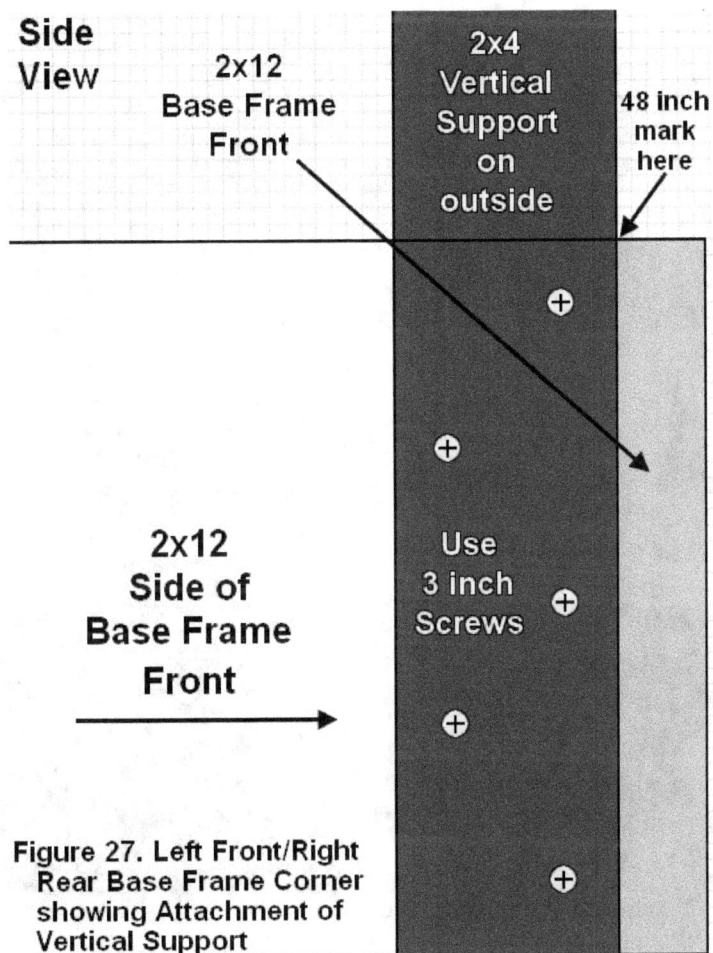

Figure 27. Left Front/Right Rear Base Frame Corner showing Attachment of Vertical Support

**Figure 28.** Left Rear/Right Front Base Frame Corner showing Attachment Vertical of Support.

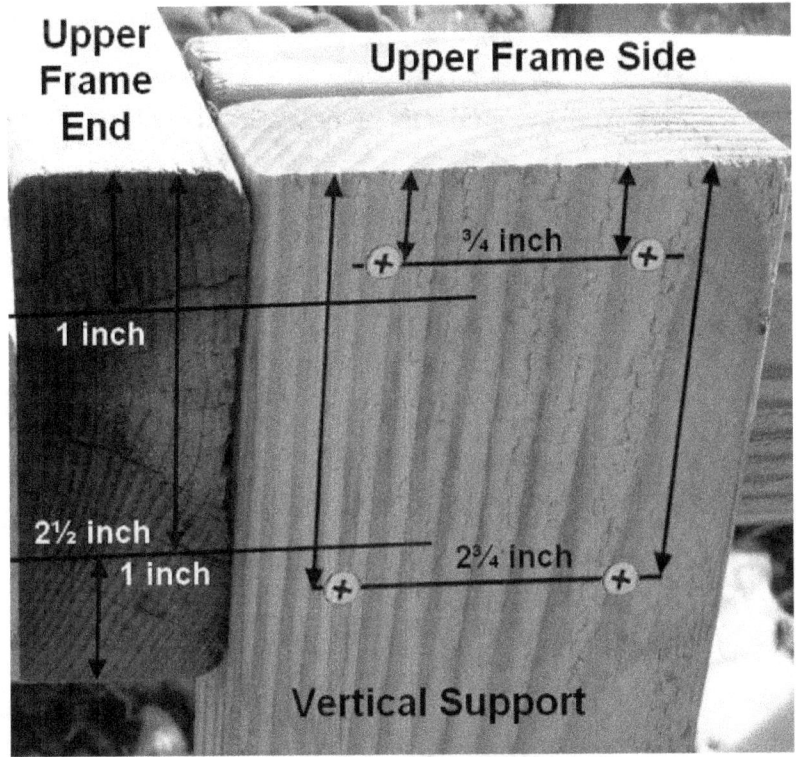

**Figure 29.** Left Front/Right Rear Corner of Upper Frame.

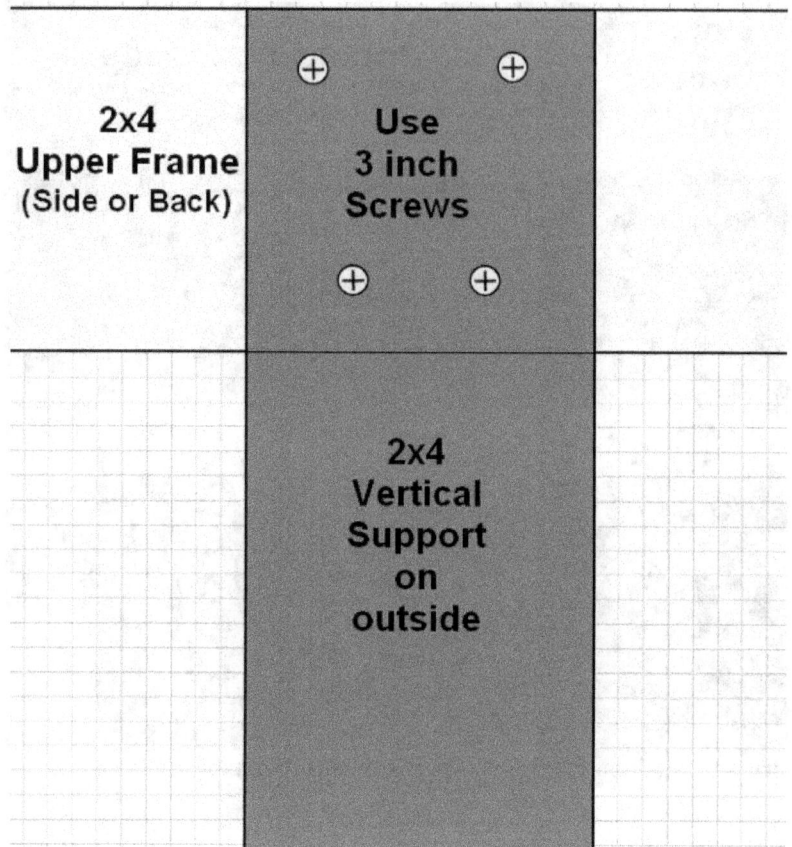

**Figure 30.** Side View - Attachment of Remaining (non-corner) Vertical Supports.

**Step 5D: Make 48 inch Marks on 4 Corner Vertical Supports**
**These 48 inch Marks are Critical for the Upper Frame to be Level.**

- If the **Base Frame is level** and
- If each of the 4 Vertical Supports are **marked at exactly 48 inches** and
- If each **mark is lined up exactly with the top of the base frame** and
- If **Vertical Supports are plumb** (level vertically - both directions)
- Then the **tops of the Vertical Supports will also be level**
- If the **Upper Frame is aligned exactly with the tops of the Vertical Supports**
- Then the **Upper Frame will be level**

The upper 48 inches will be the height at the top of the Frame above the Base Frame. The remaining 11¼ inches will be attached to the Base Frame 2x12. The marks will line up with the top of the Base Frame. These four boards will be attached close to the four corners of the Base Frame.

**Hint:** To make sure the lines are the same on each Vertical Support, line them up together on a flat surface (narrow sides up) and make all of the 48 inch marks across all boards at the same time. Make sure all the boards and marks line up. Make the marks on the sides (narrow side) of the supports so they are easier to visually line up with the top of the Base Frame.

**Step 5E: Attach 4 Vertical Supports to Base Frame Corners** - We know that "2X" lumber is really 1.5 inches thick, so when attaching two 1½ inch pieces together, the screws can only be 2¾ - 3 inches long. In fact, 3 inch screws may still poke out a little on the side unless they are at a slight angle. So remember to use 3 inch screws when fastening two 2x's flat-ways and 3.5 inch screws when at least one board is "long-ways" as shown in Figure 31.

**Hint:** I used clamps (spring clamps and/or large "C-clamp") to hold the Vertical Supports in position while I lined up the marks with the top of the Base Frame and the edge of the Vertical Support with the edge of the Base Frame side. I also plumbed the Vertical Supports before tightening any screws.

If you don't have clamps, a single screw can hold the board in position and still allow you to plumb the board as long as the board is lined up properly with the marks.

**Note:** The 4 Vertical Supports could be attached in the exact corners of the frame. They could also be attached on either the inside or the outside of the base frame, but I found that if they were offset by the thickness of the end 2x12 from the corner and were placed on the outside of the frame, there are three advantages:

1. It creates a stronger corner of the Upper Frame
2. It was easier to attach the plastic sheeting
3. The Vertical Supports are outside of the constant dripping and humidity
4. Less wear on the plastic sheeting because less wind inside the greenhouse to blow plastic into the Vertical Supports

**Step 5E: Attach 4 Vertical Supports to Base Frame Corners consists of 3 tasks:**

- **1: Clamp the Vertical Supports into Position** - or attach with a single screw or prop on temporary nails. As mentioned above, it is critical that these boards are straight vertically and are lined up exactly so the tops of the Vertical Supports are exactly 48 inches above the Base Frame.
- **2: Final Check for Alignment and Plumb** - Use a carpenters level to make sure the Vertical Supports are perfectly straight and double check that they are aligned along the ends of the Base Frame and that the 48 inch line is perfectly aligned at the top of the Base Frame.
- **3: Drive and Tighten Screws** - When the boards are plumbed and lined up properly. Place 3 inch screws into the holes already drilled into the bottom of the Vertical Supports and drive them in securely.

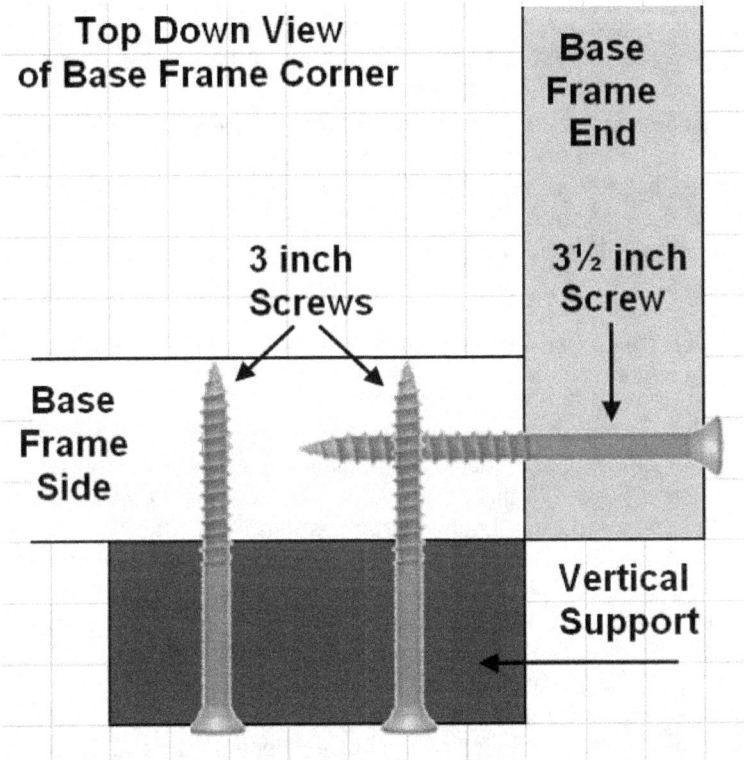

**Figure 31.** Top View of Left Front/Right Rear Corner of Base Frame.

**Step 5F: Attach Two Upper Frame End Pieces to Vertical Supports Hint:** I used clamps to hold boards in position before attaching with screws. It is easiest to start with the shorter, lighter 99 inch front and back pieces. Then add the longer, heavier 10 foot (120 inch) boards on the sides.

**Note:** We could have built and attached the 2x4s of the Upper Frame to the four corner Vertical Supports exactly as with the 2x12s of the Base Frame, but by using longer boards and cutting them to 99 inches, we can overlap the Vertical Supports and create stronger corners, because each corner is held by 8 screws. The Base Frame does not need stronger corners because it is anchored in the soil.

**To Attach Two Upper Frame End Pieces to Vertical Supports, (Step 5F) there are 4 tasks:**

- **1: Clamp Upper Frame Ends to Vertical Supports** - or let the frame piece rest on temporary nails. The ends of the 99 inch frame section should be aligned flush with the outside edge of the Vertical Supports and the top of the frame section should be aligned flush with the top edge of the Vertical Supports. Refer to Figure 32 and Fig. 33 for attaching the front and back Upper Frame pieces to the Vertical Supports.
- **2: Final Check for Alignment and Plumb** - With the frame section temporarily clamped or resting in position, double check for alignment and check plumb with carpenter's level.
- **3: Pre-drill holes** - If firmly clamped to the Vertical Support, holes can be pre-drilled in place through the end of the upper frame and into the center of the Vertical Support. Mark and pre-drill two holes, 1 inch from the top and 2½ inches from the top (or 1 inch from the bottom) as shown in Figure 32 and Fig. 33.
- **4: Drive and Tighten Screws** - When satisfied the piece is aligned properly, start and drive the two 3½ inch screws all the way in. Install the other end of the Upper Frame the same way.

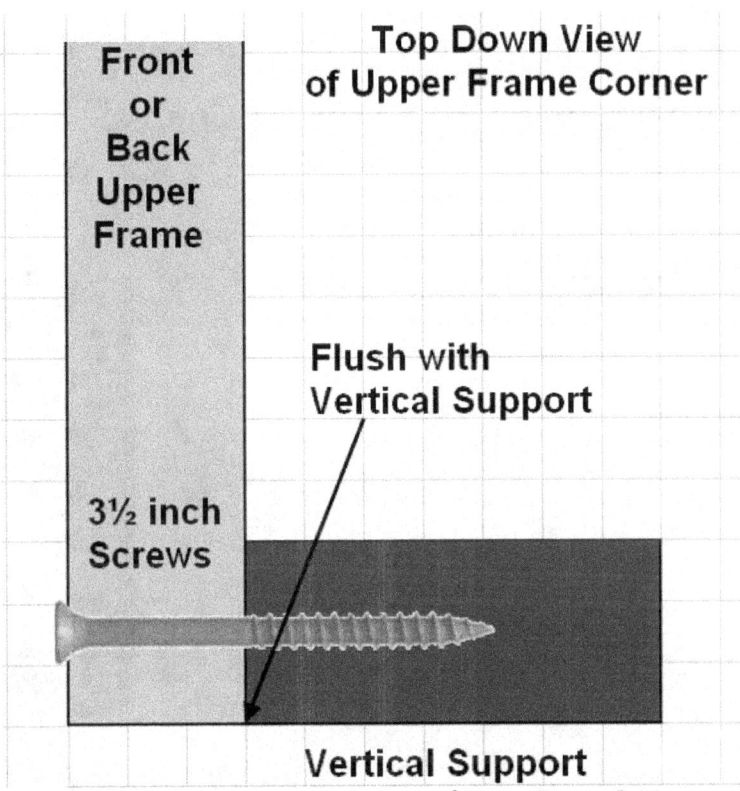

**Figure 32.** Top View - Left Front/Right Rear of Upper Frame Corner Attachment to Vertical Support.

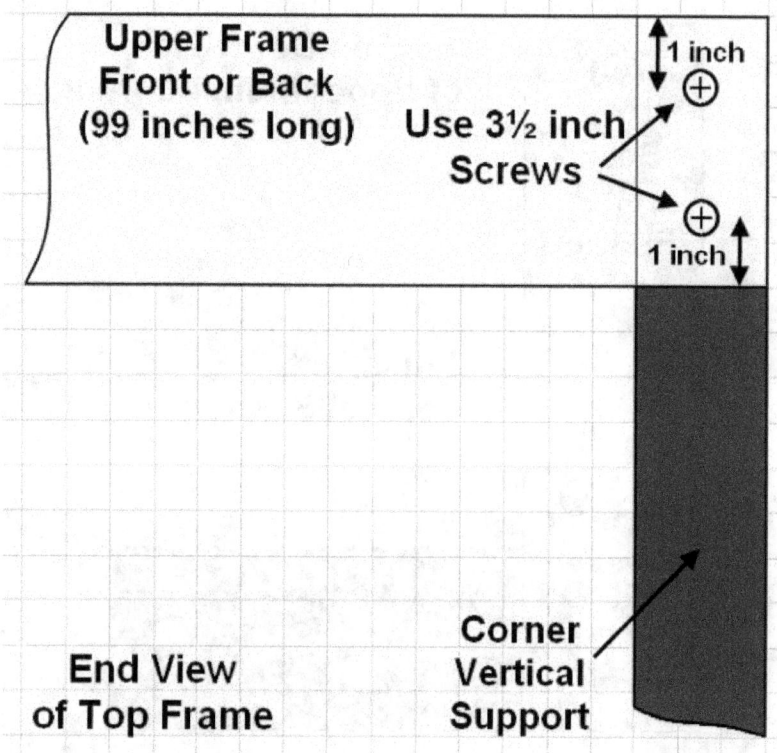

**Figure 33.** End View of Right Front/Left Rear Corner of Upper Frame Attachment to Vertical Support.

**Step 5G: Attach Two Upper Frame Side Pieces to Upper Frame End Pieces and to Vertical Supports** Now that the end pieces of the Upper Frame have been attached, continue to use clamps or nails to temporarily support the 10 foot long Upper Frame side pieces to first the Vertical supports, then to the Upper Frame end pieces.

**To Attach Two Upper Frame Side Pieces to Upper Frame End Pieces and to Vertical Supports, (Step 5G) there are 5 tasks:**

- **1: Clamp Upper Frame Sides to the Upper Frame Ends and/or to the Vertical Supports** - Notice in Figure 34 that the Upper Frame sides are attached inside of the Vertical Supports and also butt against the Upper Frame Ends that were just attached. This can also be seen in Figure 29 and Fig. 34.
- **2: Final Check for Alignment and Plumb** - With the frame section temporarily clamped or resting in position, double check for alignment and check for plumb (straight up and down) with carpenter's level and make sure the upper frame side piece is flush with the tops of the vertical supports and the upper frame end pieces.
- **3: Drive and Tighten Screws** - Using 3 inch screws, drive screws into the pre-drilled holes in the top of the Vertical Support into the Upper Frame Side piece.
- **4: Pre-drill holes** - If firmly clamped in place, holes can be pre-drilled in place through the Upper Frame end and into the center of the the Upper Frame side. Mark and pre-drill two holes, 1 inch from the top and 2½ inches from the top (or 1 inch from the bottom) as shown in Figure 35 and Fig. 36. Drill two holes, one above the other as shown in the End View of Fig. 36.
- **5: Drive and Tighten Screws** - When satisfied the piece is aligned properly, drive the two 3½ inch screws all the way in. Install the other side of the Upper Frame the same way.

**Figure 34.** Top View of Finished Left Front/Right Rear Corner of Upper Frame.

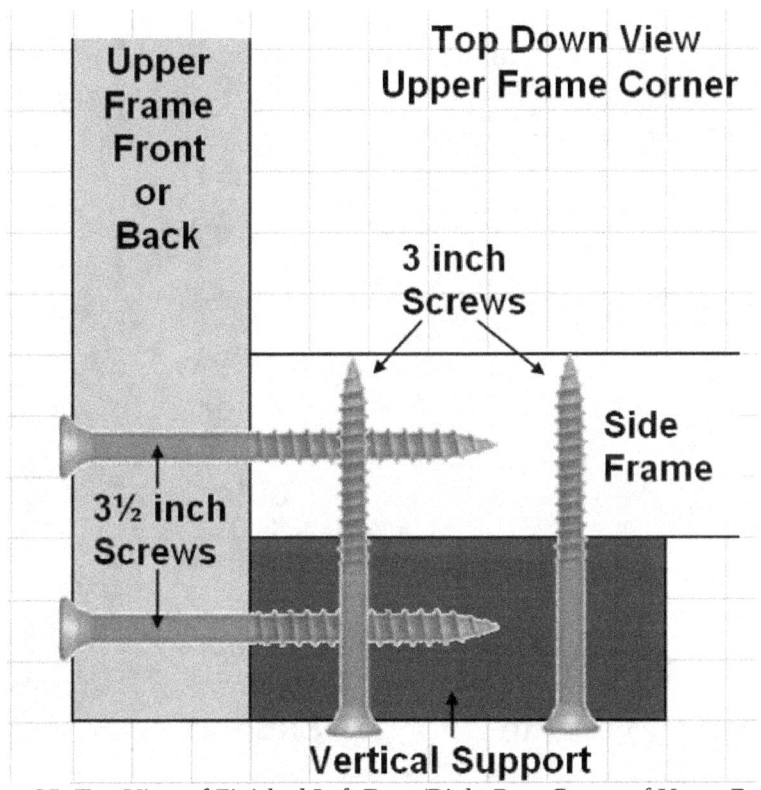

**Figure 35.** Top View of Finished Left Front/Right Rear Corner of Upper Frame.

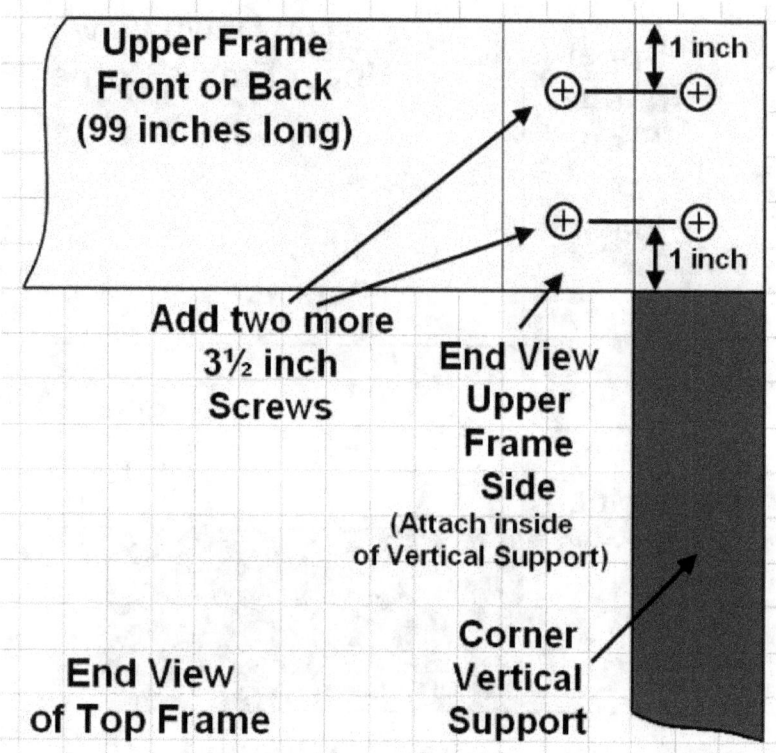

**Figure 36.** End View of Finished Right Front/Left Rear Corner of Upper Frame.

**Step 5H: Attach Remaining Vertical Supports** After the Upper Frame is attached to the 4 corner Vertical Supports, we can attach the 5 remaining Vertical Supports, with two on each side and one on the end (6 supports if you decided on two supports on the back). You should have already marked the Base Frame where the Vertical Supports should attach. Since the Base Frame is Level, we do not need to mark the Upper Frame, we simply line the supports up on the layout marks on the base frame and make sure they are flush on top with the Upper Frame and make sure they are perfectly straight.

**To Attach the Two Remaining Vertical Supports, (Step 5H) there are 3 tasks:**

- **1: Clamp Vertical Supports to Upper Frame** - make sure the Vertical Supports line up the with the layout marks on the base frame. Also line the tops of the Vertical Supports so they are flush with the top of the Side or End pieces of the Upper Frame, then check plumb with carpenters level.
- **2: Final Check for Alignment and Plumb** - With the frame section temporarily clamped or resting in position, double check for alignment and check for plumb.
- **3: Start and Tighten Screws** - When satisfied the piece is aligned properly, start the screws in the holes pre-drilled during Step 5C-4 (Fig. 30) and drive the four 3 inch screws all the way in. Install the other four Vertical Supports along the side and end of the Upper Frame the same way.

## Step 6: Build the Door Frame

Marking the Layout for the Door Frame was included in the last chapter, but if you have not yet marked the layout for the width of the door, the first step will be to mark the proper layout on the Base Frame. Measure and mark one-half the width of the door on each side of the Center Mark on the top of the Base Frame.

The Door Frame pieces are all the same size regardless of the width of the door frame you choose. In addition to framing the door, these pieces also help strengthen the entire greenhouse frame and also provide a place to attach the angled roof later.

### Steps to Building the Door Frame

[Step 6A: Mark and Cut Door Frame](#)
[Step 6B: Attach Door Frame Sides to Base Frame and Upper Frame](#)
[Step 6C: Attach Door Frame Top to Door Frame Sides](#)

### Step 6A: Mark and Cut Door Frame

Three pieces make up the door frame; two door frame sides and a door frame top (See [Table 2](#)).

### To Mark and Cut Lumber for the Door Frame, (Step 6A) there are 3 tasks:

- **1: Mark and Cut Lumber for Door Frame Sides** - Cut two 86¾ inch boards from two 2x4 studs for the side pieces.
- **2: Mark and Cut Door Frame Top**- There is only one piece to cut for the door frame top. Cut the 48 inch top frame piece from the 60 inch scrap piece leftover from cutting the vertical supports.
- **3: Mark Center and Layout on Top Door Frame Piece** - The top Door Frame piece needs to be centered on the vertical door frame side pieces. Mark this piece the same as the layout marks made for the door on the Base Frame. Measure and mark the center at 24 inches, then mark half the width of the door on each side of the center mark. The side door frame pieces line up with the marks on the bottom and line up with the same lines marked on the top door frame piece.

**Step 6B: Attach Door Frame Sides to Base Frame and Upper Frame**

The sides of the door frame are attached to the base frame exactly as the vertical supports and the sides of the door frame are also attached to the upper frame the same as the vertical supports except they extend 24 inches above the upper frame.

**To Attach Door Frame Sides to the Base Frame and the Upper Frame, (Step 6B) there are 4 tasks:**

- **1: Clamp Door Frame Side to the Upper Frame** - One at a time, make sure the Door Frame pieces are aligned properly on the layout marks on the front of the Base Frame. The Door Frame pieces are placed inside the Upper and Base Frames as shown in Fig. 37 and Fig. 38.
- **2: Final Check for Alignment and Plumb** - With the Door Frame side section temporarily clamped or held in position, double check for alignment and check for plumb.
- **3: Pre-drill holes** - While firmly clamped or held in place, holes can be pre-drilled through the Door Frame into the Base Frame and the Upper Frame. Drill 5 holes at the bottom into the Base Frame just as you did with the Vertical Supports (see Fig. 27 and Fig. 28). Drill 4 holes into the Upper Frame just as you did with the 5 Remaining Vertical Supports (Fig. 30).
- **4: Start and Tighten Screws** - When satisfied the piece is aligned properly, start and drive the four 3 inch screws all the way in. Install the other side of Door Frame the same way.

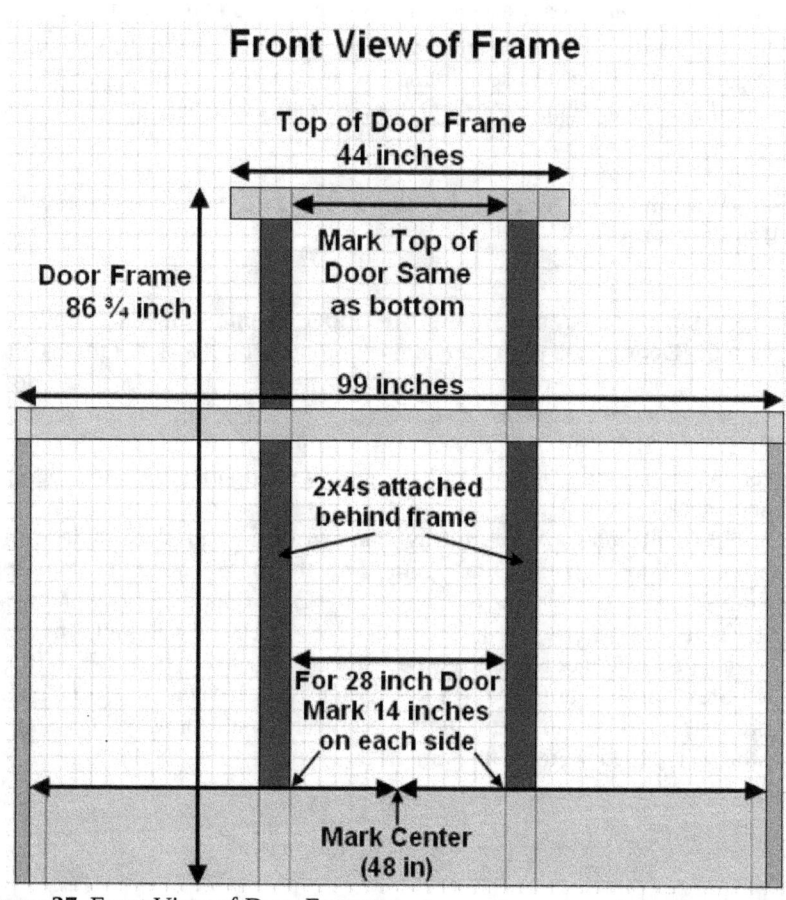

**Figure 37.** Front View of Door Frame.

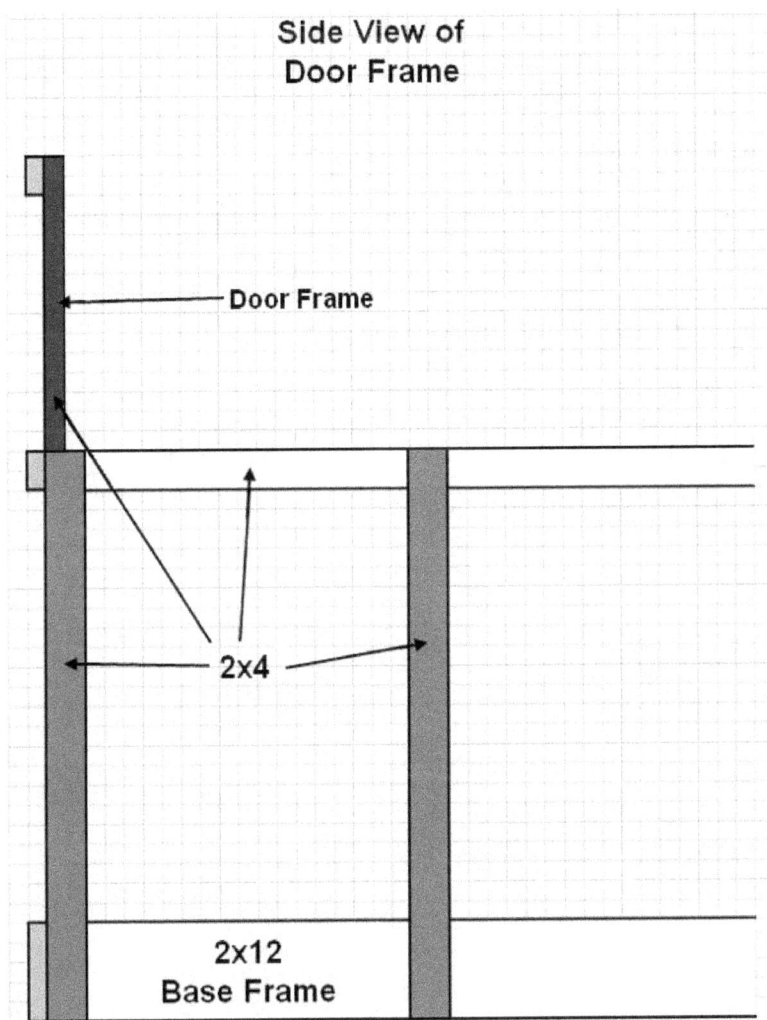

**Figure 38.** Side View of Door Frame.

**Step 6C: Attach Door Frame Top to Door Frame Sides** - Make sure to align the marks on the Top Door Frame piece properly with the door frame sides, so the door frame top is centered (Figure 37 and Fig. 39). Also make sure to place the top of the door frame in front of the frame sides (Fig. 38) and make sure the top is flush with the tops of the door frame sides.

**To Attach the top of the Door Frame to the Door Frame Sides, (Step 6C) there are 3 tasks:**

- **1: Final Check for Alignment and Level** - With the top of the door frame section clamped in position, double check for alignment and level.
- **2: Pre-drill holes** - While firmly clamped in place, holes can be pre-drilled through the top of the door frame into the door frame sides.
- **3: Start and Tighten Screws** - When satisfied the piece is aligned properly, start and drive the four 3 inch screws all the way in on both sides.

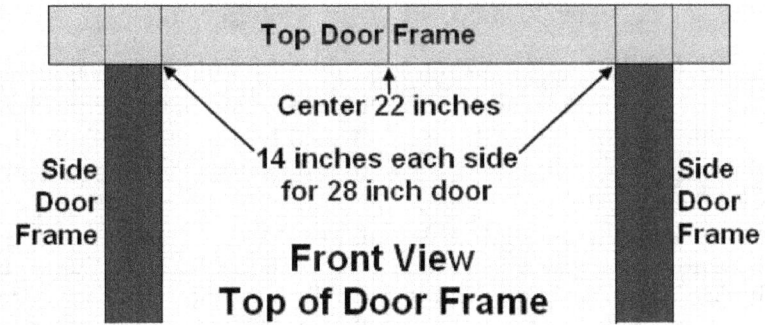
**Figure 39.** Front View of Top of Door Frame.

### Step 7: Build and Attach Roof Section

The wooden roof angle has the only 45° cut in the entire greenhouse project. This is a fairly simple cut with most circular or hand saws, but if you are not able to make this cut, I offer an alternative in Step 7A below. The wood roof section adds stability to the door frame and gives the front of the greenhouse a traditional gable shape.

After the roof section is installed, the last step in this section is to remove the upper frame section that is blocking the door frame. This step is last since a strong upper frame helps keep everything sturdy until the door frame and roof angles are attached. See the diagrams in Figure 40 and Fig. 41 and also the picture in Fig. 24.

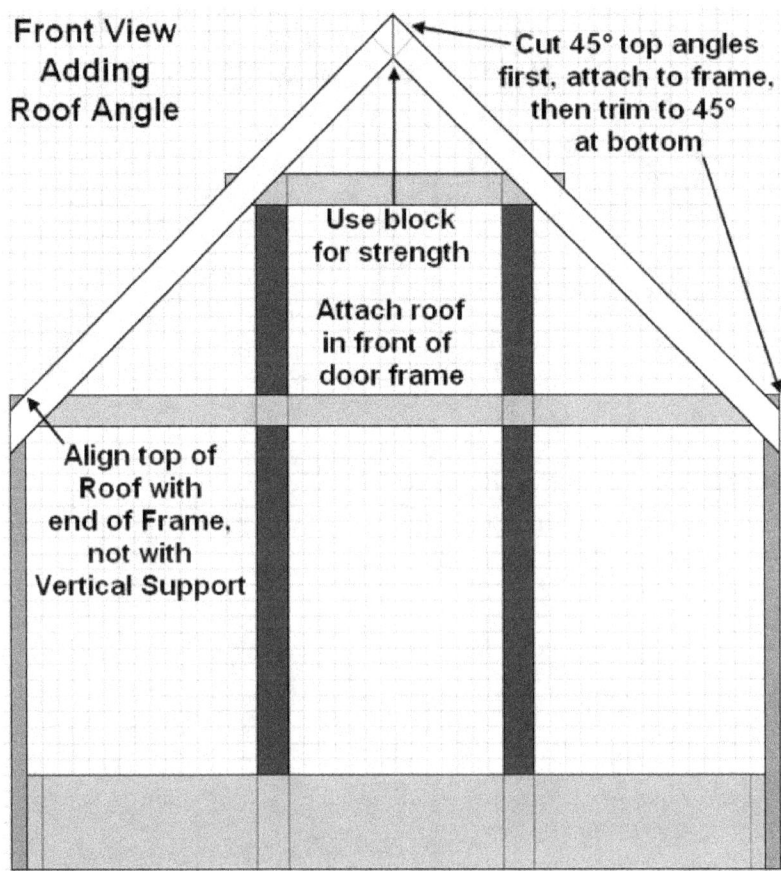

**Figure 40.** Front View of Attached Roof Section.

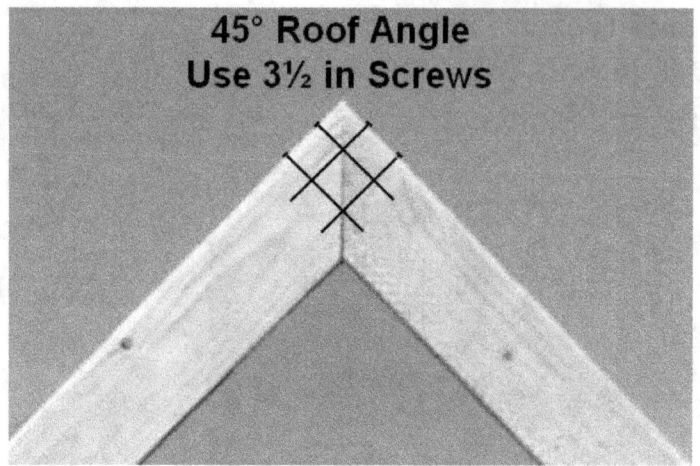

**Figure 41.** Front View of 45° Roof Peak.

**Steps to Building the Roof Angles**
Step 7A: Make Two 45° Cuts
Step 7B: Join the Roof Angles
Step 7C: Strengthen Joint
Step 7A-7C Alternate Method
Step 7D: Make Reference Marks on Roof Section
Step 7E: Clamp the Roof Section into Place
Step 7F: Final Check for Alignment
Step 7G: Mark and Pre-drill Holes
Step 7H: Attach Roof Section
Step 7I: Trim Ends of the Roof Flush

**Step 7A: Make Two 45° Cuts** - Starting with two uncut 8 foot 2x4s, Mark the 45° angles on one end of each board. Make these cuts and remove as little length of these boards as possible. The scrap from these boards will be used to fill in the door frame later. If you are not experienced making 45° cuts with a circular saw, practice on scrap wood to learn how to line the saw up properly on the marks with the blade angled. If you are not comfortable making this cut, you can use the Alternate Method. For reference, see the Roof Section in Figure 24, Fig. 40 and Fig. 41.

**Step 7B: Join the Roof Angles** - If satisfied with 45° cuts, pre-drill two holes in each board from the top into the cut of the other board as shown in Figure 41. If you already have wood glue, it wouldn't hurt to apply some to both joint surfaces before driving the four 3½ inch screws down tight.

**Step 7C: Strengthen Joint** - The joint should be strengthened whether you used glue or not. The joint is strengthened by using tie plates or a 3½ inch block cut from a 2x4 as shown in Figure 42. Attach the Tie plate or block across the joint with additional screws. If using the block, use 3 inch screws. If using a tie plate, use screws that will not stick out the opposite side.

**Figure 42.** Rear View of Roof Peak. Showing block used to strengthen the joint. A Furring Strip remains on the left side where plastic was attached.

**Step 7A-7C Alternate Method for Building 45° Roof Angle** - This is a simple method to create the 45° roof angle, but requires a tie plate or an additional block and 6 bolts (3/8 or 1/4 inch), 12 washers and 6 nuts.

- **1: Line Two Boards up at 45° Angle** - Line the two uncut 8 foot 2x4s up as shown in Figure 43.
- **2: Joint Roof Sections with Tie Plate or Block** - Use one or two tie plates or cut a 7 inch block from a scrap 2x4 and line the block or plate up over the joint as shown in Figure 44.
- **3: Mark and/or Drill Holes** - Most Tie plates will already be pre-drilled, so lined the tie plate up over the joint and mark holes to be drilled. Drill at least 3 holes on each board the same size as the bolts. If using a scrap block, line the block up over the joint with a scrap block underneath. Drill holes all the way through the block and the roof section.
- **4: Attach with Bolts** - Insert Bolts with washer through the block or Tie plates and holes in the roof sections. Put another washer on the bolt and tighten nuts.

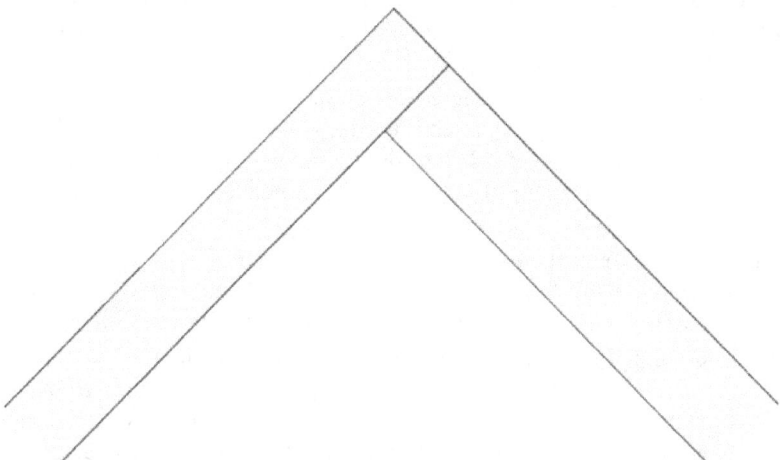

**Figure 43.** Step 1 of Alternate Method for Constructing 45° Roof Peak. Line Boards up to Create 45° Angle.

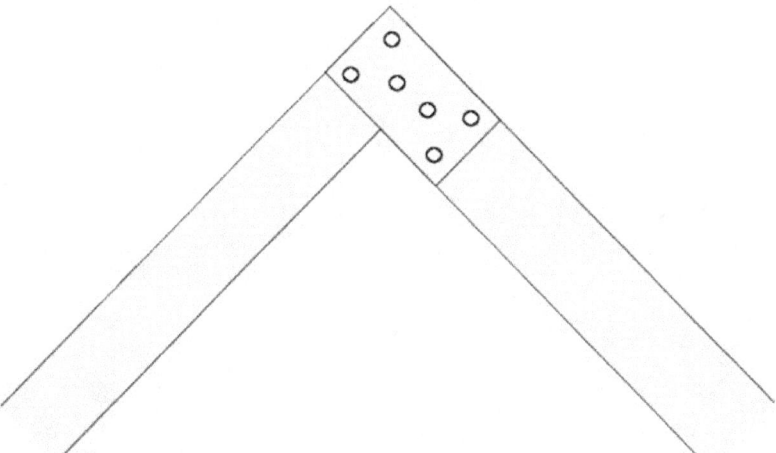

**Figure 44.** Step 2 of Alternate Method for Constructing 45° Roof Peak. Roof Angles are joined with Tie-plate or block with bolts.

**Step 7D: Make Reference Marks on Roof Section** - Before Clamping the Roof into place, we need to make some reference marks so we can center the roof section when we clamp it in place.

Since the roof section is a 45° degree angle, the rise is 48 inches from the top of the upper frame to the roof peak and the run is 48 inches from the edge of the upper frame to the center of the door frame. Using basic trigonometry ($A^2+B^2=C^2$), C, or the length from the roof peak to the edge of the upper frame is equal to 67.88 inches.

So measure from the peak along the top edge of the roof section (on both sides) and make marks at 67¾ and 68 inches. 67.88 inches is in between those two marks, so the first mark is a little short and the second mark is a little long.

**Step 7E: Clamp the Roof Section into Place** - Clamp the roof section to the front side of the upper frame and/or to the top of the door frame as shown in Figure 45. The roof section should be as close to center as possible, so that the roof peak is dead center of the door frame. Line the reference marks (from Step 7D) up with the top and outside edges of the Upper Frame on both sides, so they are as equal as possible. This method may not be close enough for fine cabinetry work, but it is close enough for the greenhouse.

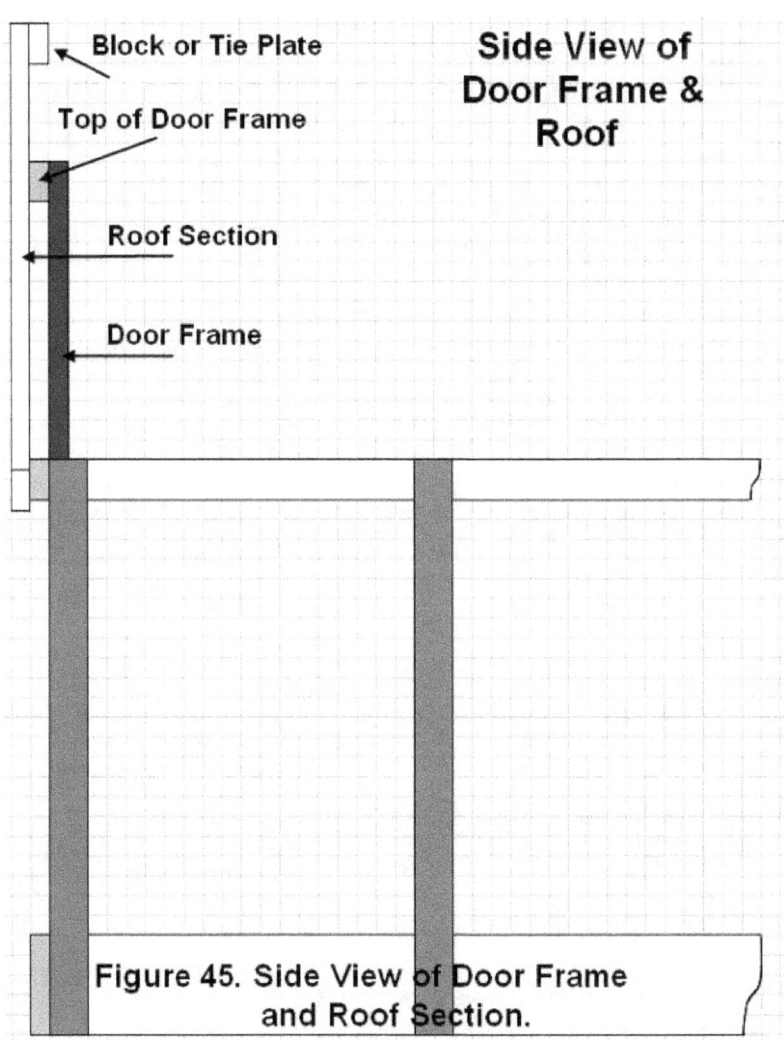

Figure 45. Side View of Door Frame and Roof Section.

**Step 7F: Final Check for Alignment** - Take one last chance to double check that the roof section is clamped on the outside of the door frame, the roof peak appears to be dead center of the door frame and the reference marks are aligned equally on both sides of the roof section with the outside edge of the upper frame.

**Step 7G: Mark and Pre-drill Holes** - While firmly clamped or held in place, holes can be pre-drilled through the top of the Door Frame and the Upper Frame. Drill 3 holes each place where the roof section contacts the roof section; both sides of tip of Door Frame and both sides of Upper Frame. Try not to drill into the screws that are already holding the frame together.

**Step 7H: Attach Roof Section** - When satisfied the roof section is aligned properly, start 3 inch screws and drive all 12 screws down tight.

**Step 7I: Trim Ends of the Roof Flush** - Now that the roof is secured, cut the long ends of the roof section flush with the corner vertical supports. I made these cuts with a hand saw, but you can make this cut with a power saw or a reciprocating saw if you feel you can do so safely.

### Step 8: Complete Door Frame

Now, we need to make the door frame easier to seal with the door and also strengthen the frame, by filling in the gaps of the door frame between the base frame and the upper frame and the gaps between the upper frame and the top of the door frame (see Figure 46, Fig. 47 and Fig. 48).

<u>Step 8A: Mark and Cut Fill Pieces</u>
<u>Step 8B: Fit Fill Pieces into Door Frame</u>
<u>Step 8C: Pre-drill Holes in Fill Pieces and Attach</u>
<u>Step 8D: Remove the Upper Frame Section from the Door Frame</u>

**Step 8A: Mark and Cut Fill Pieces** - If these pieces were previously cut back in Step 5, there should be two 44½ inch pieces and two 24 inch pieces that were cut a bit long for a tight fit.

If not previously cut, mark and cut two 44½ inch pieces from a 2x4 stud and two 24 inch pieces from scrap from the roof section. Cut all of these so they will fit very tightly.

**Step 8B: Fit Fill Pieces into Door Frame** - Then test the four pieces and see how tight they are. Obviously, the two long 44½ inch pieces fill in the lower part of the door frame and the two 24 inch pieces fill in the upper part of the door frame as previously mentioned in Figure 46, Fig. 47 and Fig. 48). Sand them or file them down until they fit tightly.

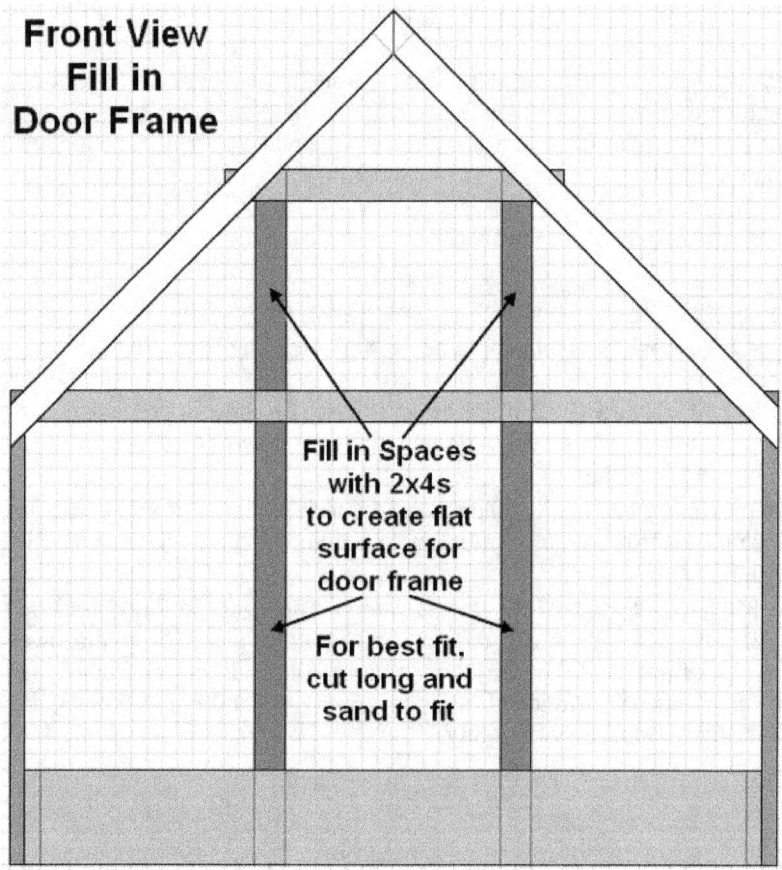

**Figure 46.** Front View showing Gaps to be Filled to Stiffen and Flush Door Frame.

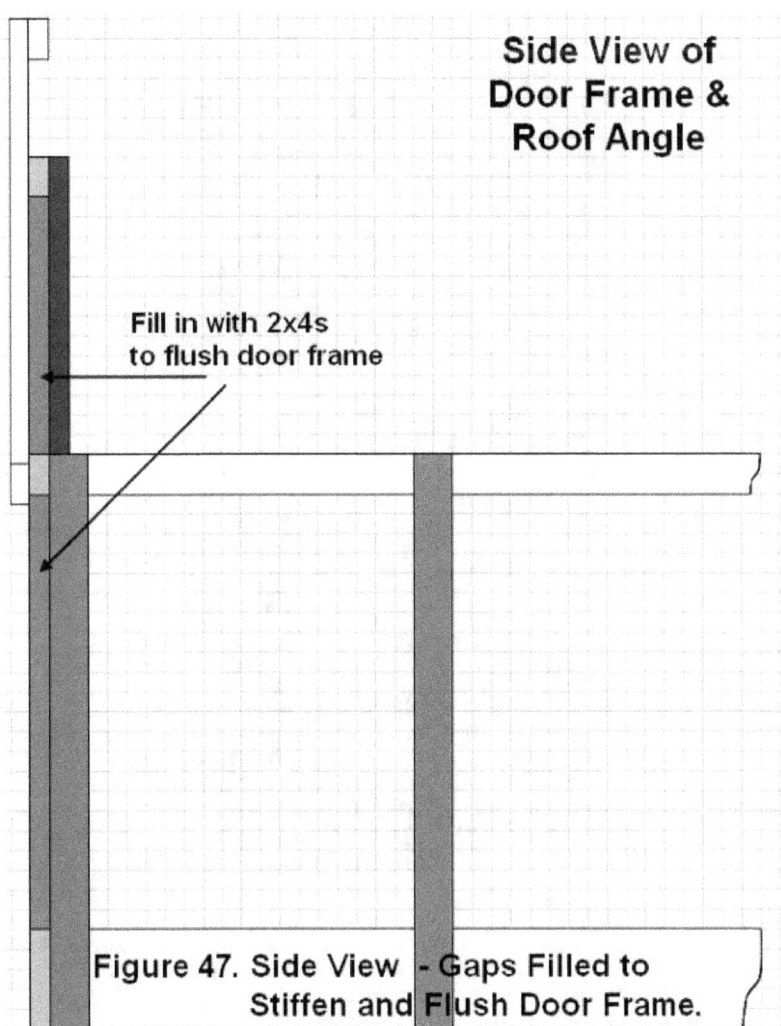

Figure 47. Side View - Gaps Filled to Stiffen and Flush Door Frame.

Figure 48. Gaps Filled in Door Frame.

**Step 8C: Pre-drill Holes in Fill Pieces and Attach** - Once the pieces are tightly in place, there should be no need to hold or clamp them. Pre-drill 3 or 4 staggered holes in the upper fill pieces and 4 or 5 holes in each lower fill piece. Use 3 inch screws and drive them into the Door Frame.

**Step 8D: Remove the Upper Frame Section from the Door Frame** - After the door frame is strengthened, remove the section of the upper frame that is blocking the door frame ([Figure 48](#) and [Fig. 49](#)). It is important to make this cut flush with the side of the door frame so the door does not stick. I made these cuts with a hand saw, but you can also make this cut with a power saw or a reciprocating saw if you feel you can do so safely.

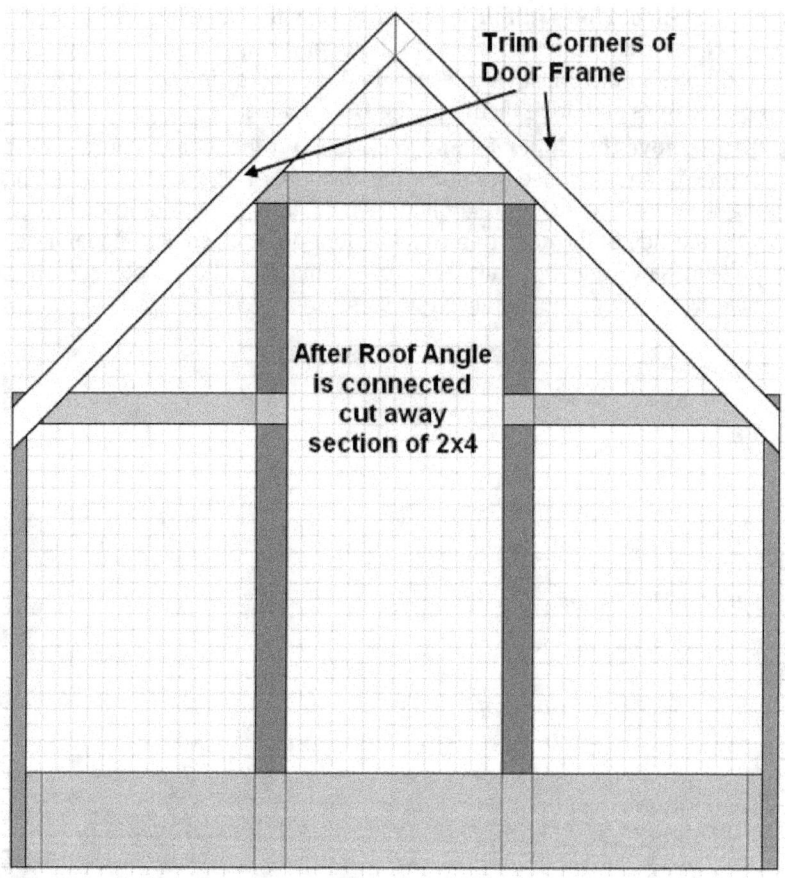

**Figure 49.** Front View - Cut-away of Frame Section from Door Frame and Trimmed Door Frame.

## Step 9: Build the PVC A-Frame Roof

The PVC Roof is simple to assemble. The entire roof consists of five PVC supports from each side. These support ribs are attached to each other at the top with zip-ties (AKA cable ties or tie wraps). Another PVC pipe is slid inside all the zip-ties before they are tightened and forms the spine or backbone of the PVC Roof.

The PVC Ribs are attached to the wooden frame with metal conduit straps, which are attached with screws to the wooden frame.

Once the conduit is in place and after the PVC pipe has been cut to length and drilled, the entire roof frame can be assembled in less than 15 minutes and can be taken down in 5 minutes.

### Steps to Building the PVC supports for the Greenhouse

[Step 9A: Mark and Attach Conduit Straps](#)
[Step 9B: Drill holes in Upper End of PVC Ribs](#)
[Step 9C: Test Two PVC Ribs to Determine Length](#)
[Step 9D: Cut PVC Pipe to Length](#)
[Step 9E: Insert PVC into Conduit Straps and Attach](#)
[Step 9F: Connect PVC Ribs with zip-ties](#)
[Step 9G: Slide PVC Spine in between zip-tie Loops](#)
[Step 9H: Attach Spine to Wooden Roof Angle](#)
[Step 9I: Adjust Ribs & Tighten zip-ties](#)

**Step 9A: Mark and Attach the Conduit Straps to the Upper Frame** - The placement of the rib supports are not critical, but it makes sense to space them evenly. The first rib support will be placed about a foot inches inside from the Center of the wood roof angle so a 24 inch piece of plastic sheeting can easily cover this gap.

The last rib support will be as close to the end of the upper frame as possible. The other 3 supports on each side will be spaced equally in between the first and last ribs.

The PVC ribs could be attached either inside or outside of the upper frame, but I think attaching the PVC inside the frame is best because it is easier to attach the plastic sheeting to the top of the wooden frame and also, the horizontal forces from the PVC ribs push into the upper frame instead of pushing against only the two screws that hold the conduit straps.

Attaching the ribs outside of the frame would provide a few more inches of room for plants, but condensation would constantly drip on the wooden frame.

**To Mark and Attach Conduit Straps to the Upper Frame, (Step 9A) there are 4 tasks:**

- **1: Mark Location for Back Conduit Straps -** On the inside of the upper frame, mark two inches from the inside back end on both sides (Fig. 50).
- **2: Mark Location for Front Conduit Straps** - Mark 8 inches from the front of the upper frame (11¾ inches from center of the roof angle) on both sides.
- **3: Mark Location for Remaining Conduit Straps -** Mark the centers for the other 3 conduit straps at 25, 50 and 75 inches from the center of either the front or back conduit straps.
- **4: Attach Conduit Straps -** Center all 10 Conduit Straps on the marks and attach each with two 1½ inch screws near the top of the upper frame.

**Figure 50.** Conduit Strap in Back Corner of Upper Frame.

**Step 9B: Drill holes in Upper End of PVC Ribs** - Drill holes in one end of each of the PVC ribs; Drill at an angle as shown in Figure 51. These holes need to be large enough for the zip-ties to thread through them. The zip-ties I used were about 3/8th inches wide, so I used a 3/8th drill bit and "wallowed" it around a bit to make the hole slightly larger. This doesn't need to be exact, but we want the zip-ties to be tight in the holes, but not too tight and we don't want the holes to be too big either.

**Figure 51.** Drill Holes at an Angle in the Top of Each PVC Rib. The hole needs to be large enough to allow the electrical zip-ties to thread through.

**Step 9C: Test Two PVC Ribs to Determine Length** - Before we cut all of the PVC pipes to make the support ribs, it is a good idea to test two of them to make sure the length is correct. The height and shape of the PVC roof is determined by the length and flexibility of the PVC pipe.

It is a simple task to determine the length of a 2x4 roof piece as long as we know the angle. It is a little more complicated to calculate the length of a piece of material that is bent into an ellipse. PVC pipe is not straight like a 2x4 and it also does not bend into a perfect ellipse, so calculating the exact length needed to cover the greenhouse is a little complicated. The PVC ribs bend like shown in the diagram (Figure 52) and the picture (Figure 23).

If the PVC pipe bent like an ellipse, the length of the PVC ribs above the frame would be 75.4 inches. If the PVC were rigid like lumber, the length would be 67.88 inches. But the PVC pipe bends, but not as much as an ellipse, so the length is somewhere in between and difficult to calculate exactly, but depending upon the flexibility of your PVC pipe, should be 70-72 inches above the frame. Adding 3½ inches for attachment to the upper frame gives a total length of 73½-75½ inches.

I cut my PVC ribs to 70 inches (total length) and the height of my PVC roof is 44 inches above the upper frame, which is 4 inches lower than the wooden roof peak as shown back in Figure 1, Fig. 2 and Fig. 3.

The PVC roof should be lower than the wooden roof peak for two reasons:

1. Higher roof requires more plastic to cover the back end
2. A lower roof reduces the wind force on the greenhouse

It also takes more plastic to cover the roof, but the roof section is not the problem. We don't save much plastic by reducing the frame height by four inches, but unless we want to buy a third roll of plastic sheeting, we need to save a few inches where we can. We need to keep the top of the PVC roof frame less than 48 inches above the frame. As you will see later, a 48 inch height leaves only 2¼ inches of extra plastic to cover the back end of the greenhouse. That is cutting it very close to be able to close this end with the homemade PVC clamps. A 44 inch height leaves an ample 6¼ inches of extra plastic sheeting.

Since PVC pipes have different strength, thickness and flexibility, you should test a pair of PVC ribs before cutting all the pipes to length.

**Test Two PVC Ribs for Final Height**

- **Attach PVC Pipes at Top** - Using zip-ties as shown in Figure 53 and Fig. 54, attach the two pipes by sliding zip-ties through the holes. Do not tighten zip-ties too much, just enough to gauge where the height of the roof.
- **Slide PVC Pipes into Conduit Straps** - Place the two PVC pipes in place with and temporarily hold with vice-grip pliers or tie with string on opposite sides of the frame. Adjust the PVC pipes up or down until they form the height and shape you want.
- **Mark PVC Pipes** - Mark both pipes at the bottom of upper frame. This is the amount you want to cut off of every pipe that will become the PVC ribs. Remember not to exceed the height of the greenhouse roof peak and that 2-4 inches shorter than the wood roof peak will be better.

**Note:** Remember, you can always cut another inch or two off, but you can't easily put a piece back. PVC pipe can be connected with PVC cement, but it will require a larger diameter connector and will be very rigid in the repaired area.

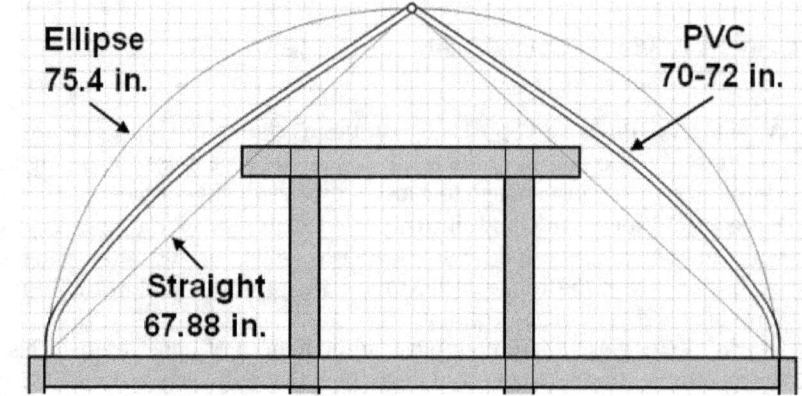

**Figure 52.** Diagram Comparing PVC A-Frame, Ellipse and Straight Line.

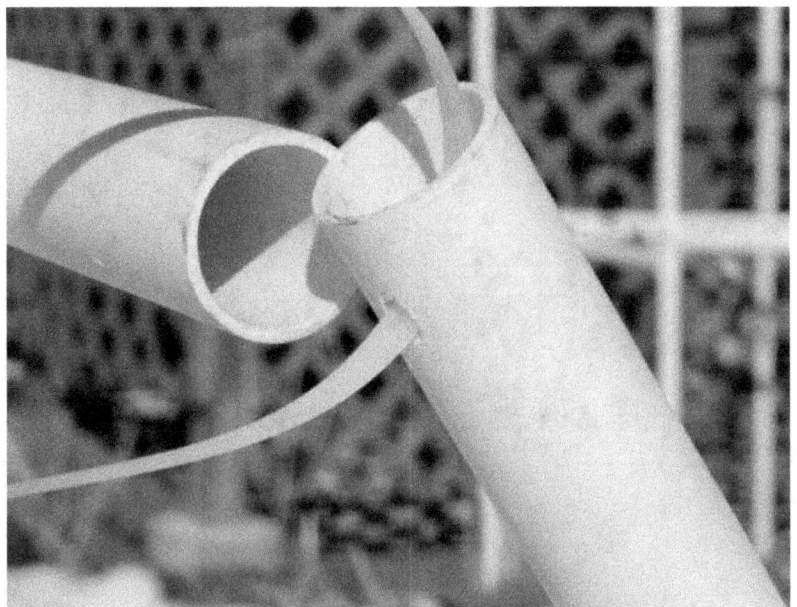

**Figure 53.** Loosely Attach Zip-ties Between Opposing PVC Ribs. Make sure to leave room to slide the spine into place.

**Figure 54.** Slide the Single Uncut 10 foot PVC Pipe (Spine) in between all Zip-ties.

**Step 9D: Cut PVC Pipe to Length** - if satisfied with the results from the first two test ribs, mark and cut the remaining eight PVC pipes to the same length. Remember to leave one PVC pipe uncut, as this will be the spine for the PVC A-frame.

**Step 9E: Insert PVC into Conduit Straps and Attach with Screws** - Insert the bottom (un-drilled end) of each PVC rib into a conduit strap and attach with a single screw as shown in Figure 55.

**Figure 55.** PVC Roof Support Ribs Attached to Upper Frame. Attached with 1 inch Conduit Strapping and Screw.

**Step 9F: Connect PVC Ribs with Zip-ties** - Loosely attach zip-ties between opposing PVC ribs. Make sure to leave room to slide spine into place (Figure 53 and Fig. 54). Zip-ties should be at least 8 inches long to be able to connect through both ends and still leave space to slide the center spine. Thread the zip-ties through the PVC so they can be tightened from below and leave a smooth surface on top for the plastic sheeting to slide over.

**Note:** I have used both UV-treated and untreated zip-ties. The untreated zip-ties lasted longer than the treated zip-ties, but the untreated zip-ties were also heavier. I never had an untreated zip-tie fail during an entire growing season, but have had to replace a few treated zip-ties. So I think it is more important to get heavy duty zip-ties instead of UV-treated zip-ties. If you notice any that have broken, simply replace them as soon as possible.

**Step 9G: Slide PVC Spine in between Zip-tie Loops** - Slide the single uncut 10 foot PVC pipe that will act as the spine in between all the zip-ties (Figure 54) and partially tighten zip-ties but do not bind the spine yet.

**Step 9H: Attach Spine to Wooden Roof Angle** - After considering all sorts of complicated methods to attach the end of the PVC spine to the wooden roof section, I finally attached it with a single screw at an angle from beneath into the block that ties the two roof angles together. If you look closely at the bottom of the block in Figure 42, you can see a ring made by the PVC spine and a screw hole in the middle of the ring.

**Step 9I: Adjust PVC Ribs & Tighten Zip-ties** - After the PVC spine is attached to the wooden roof angle, it is time to adjust the ribs and tighten the Zip-ties. But now that the Top of the PVC A-frame is about 8 feet high, you will need a ladder to safely reach the top.

**To Adjust the PVC Ribs & Tighten the Zip-ties, (Step 9I) there are 3 tasks:**

- **Adjust Rib Pairs** - Slide pairs of ribs up or back along the PVC spine so they are as vertical as possible..
- **Tighten Zip-ties** - Partially tighten zip-ties by hand and make sure the spine is resting on top of each rib as shown in Figure 56 and Fig. 57. The PVC structure is stronger this way, and it also provides a smooth surface for plastic sheeting.

- **Double Check Alignment** - If satisfied the PVC Ribs are straight and the PVC spine is on top, completely tighten all the zip-ties until the spine is held firmly in place, using pliers if needed. **Note:** If the zip-ties bind too much, you may need to drill the holes slightly larger. Also, be careful when use pliers to pull zip-ties tight as using too much force will break them.

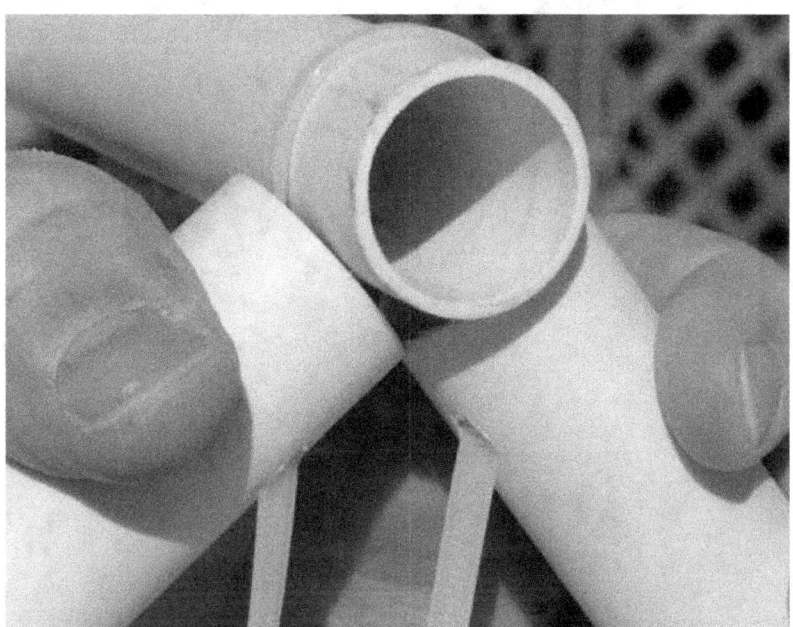

**Figure 56.** Slowly Tighten all Zip-ties. Tighten a little at a time. Make sure the spine (top support) is on top and not trapped between the ribs.

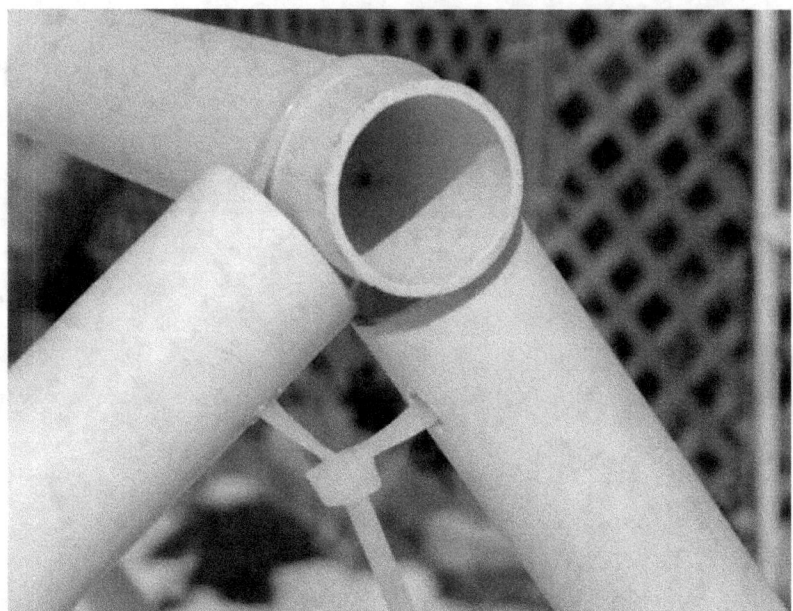

**Figure 57.** Final Configuration of PVC Spine and Support Ribs. Completely tighten all the zip-ties until the spine is held firmly in place.

### Step 10: Save $ - Make Your Own PVC Clamps

Specially made 4 inch PVC clamps can be purchased that clamps onto PVC pipe, but clamps can also be easily made from scrap sections of the same size PVC pipe used to build the greenhouse. If you plan on buying PVC clamps, skip forward to STEP 11. So, whenever I refer to PVC clamps it can be either homemade or "store-bought" clamps.

The clamps are made by basically splitting and then removing a small section (½ inch) of material along the entire length from a short section of PVC pipe as shown in Figure 58.

**Figure 58.** Homemade PVC Clamps. Use for attaching plastic sheeting to the PVC Frame.

## Steps to Make homemade PVC Clamps
Step 10A: Cut PVC Pipe
Step 10B: Remove Section of PVC Pipe

**Step 10A: Cut PVC Pipe** - Cut sections of PVC pipe into various lengths from 3-6 inches long. Longer pieces are very strong and hold well, but they are also very hard to put on and to take off. Pieces with narrow slits are also harder to put on and take off, but hold better than pieces with wider slits.

Long pieces also do not work well on the curved lower surface of the A-frame, so you will want to make several short pieces. You will want at least 16 clamps; four clamps to hold the plastic sheeting onto the PVC frame on each side and at at each end.

**Note:** I like to have an extra pair of clamps for attaching the roof section near the peak, so when I want to ventilate the back, I don't have to re-clamp the roof section right away. When I re-attach the back to close the vent, I replace the clamps, so I suggest making 18 clamps.

**Step 10B: Remove Section of Pipe** - Once you have PVC pieces of various lengths, secure them in a vise or jig so you can cut out the middle section without cutting yourself. I found it easiest to secure the pieces in a vise and score them deeply with a hack saw or key-hole saw. Because the pipe is rounded, it is easiest to make cuts with the saw on the inside of the pipe and cut toward the outside. I complete the cuts with a sharp lock-blade knife. It may seem like the cuts could be made with a good utility knife, but I could not make the cuts straight enough.

**Note:** I strongly advise against splitting PVC pipe with utility knife because it seems too dangerous to me. It would also be simple and safe to split the PVC pipe with a table saw using a guide and a push stick.

**Note:** Be advised that when you saw PVC pipe, lots of electrostatic PVC granules are created that stick to everything.

**Note:** My wife developed a simple method to attach the homemade clips that prevents getting your fingers pinched. "Real men" can attach and remove the clamps without the "finger savers", but I started using them because they also help to protect the plastic sheeting. I have to admit, I got tired of getting "blood blisters". To make the finger savers, cut two short sections, about 3 inches long from on old garden hose and split them as shown in Figure 59.

**Figure 59.** Homemade "Finger Savers". Cut from on old garden hose for attaching PVC clamps to PVC frame.

Figure 63, Fig. 64 and Fig. 65 in Step 11 below give directions for using the "finger savers" to attach the plastic sheeting to the PVC frame.

## Step 11: Cover the Greenhouse

In Section III, I have included some Additional Greenhouse Covering Materials and Additional Methods for Attaching Plastic Sheeting to the Greenhouse, but for now, I am still use utility grade Plastic Sheeting (Figure 93) to cover the Greenhouse. This plastic is not UV protected, so it only lasts one growing season. Read Notes about Plastic Sheeting to see why I still use utility grade Plastic Sheeting and how to make the plastic last longer.

The Plastic Sheeting is attached to the Greenhouse in two ways:

1. Furring strips are wrapped in plastic sheeting and screwed to the wooden frame
2. PVC clamps hold plastic sheeting to PVC ribs (roof only)

One of the simplest methods I have used to attach the plastic sheeting to the wood frame of the greenhouse is to roll a wooden furring strip in the plastic so it is wrapped at least one and half times to two times around the furring strip. This creates a strong attachment point that so far (knock on wood), has never failed despite strong wind and heavy snow..

**Note:** I have been tempted to use a special batten material used by commercial greenhouses instead of the furring strips, but I can only find it online, so shipping rates are high and it has to be purchased in large rolls. Since my original furring strips are still good, I continue to use them.

I don't think think it matters in what particular order the different sections of plastic sheeting are attached to the green house, but I do think it is easiest to put the roof section on before putting up side or end panels, because they block your movement.

The panels help block the wind, so it may help to start up wind and work down wind. but it the greenhouse can get warm on a sunny day, so you may want a breeze. I always start with the largest sections first starting with the roof.

There are two basic rules that make this method of attaching plastic sheeting work well.

1. The furring strips should be cut a few inches shorter (on each side) than the

gap being covered because we need room to work.
2. The plastic sheeting has to be cut longer than the gap in all directions (if possible), so there is room to wrap the plastic around the furring strip and for extra plastic to overlap in the corners.

<u>**Step 11A: Measure & Cut Furring Strips**</u>
<u>**Step 11B: Measure & Cut Plastic Sheeting**</u>
<u>**Step 11C: Clamp Plastic Sheeting to PVC Ribs**</u>
<u>**Step 11D: Wrap Furring Strip with Plastic Sheeting and Attach to Frame**</u>
<u>**Step 11E: Secure Inside Corners & Sides of Door Frame**</u>
<u>**Step 11F: Seal Gaps**</u>

**Step 11A: Measure & Cut Furring Strips** - <u>Table 3</u> shows all the necessary furring strips needed to attach the plastic sheeting to the greenhouse. Furring strips come in 8 foot sections, so six pieces do not need to be cut.

**Table 3. Cut List for Furring Strips for 8x10 foot Greenhouse**

| Furring Strip Cut List | | | |
|---|---|---|---|
| Furring Strips | Cut (in) | Num Pieces | Application |
| 4 | uncut | 4 | 2 Sides; top & bottom |
| 2 | uncut | 2 | Roof; top of frame |
| 2 | 92 | 2 | Back; top & bottom |
| 2 | 64 | 2 | 2 Roof Section; top |
| 1 | 24 | 2 | 2 Front Lower Panels; bottom |
| 1 | 30 | 2 | 2 Front Triangles; top |
| 2 | 70 | 2 | Door Frame |
| 2 | 44 | 4 | 4 Vertical Corners |
| scrap | 32 | 1 | Top of Door Frame |
| scrap | 20 | 3 | Vent; 2 sides, bottom |
| scrap | 8 | 2 | Roof Strip - top of frame |
| scrap | 26½ | 2 | Door; top & bottom |
| 1 | 72 | 1 | Door; outside edge |
| scrap | 48 | 1 | Door; inside edge |

**Step 11B: Measure & Cut Plastic Sheeting** - It takes two 10x25 foot rolls of 6 mil Utility Plastic Sheeting (see Materials List) to cover the greenhouse.

**Note:** It is more economical to buy the plastic sheeting in 100 foot rolls, but the 10x25 foot rolls are available at many places. Also, rolls are available in sizes wider than 10 feet.

Table 4 shows all the pieces of plastic sheeting needed to cover the greenhouse and Figure 60 shows where the more complicated cuts fit on the greenhouse. The remaining cuts; roof, sides and back should be self explanatory.

Figures 61 and Fig. 62 show how to cut the pieces from the two rolls. These cuts are designed to leave plenty of extra plastic to be able to wrap the furring strips before attaching it.

- **Measure** - Measure and mark on both sides of the plastic to be cut.
- **Fold & Secure** - You do not need to draw a line, but simply fold the plastic between the two measured points and this will create the line to cut. Weight the plastic down with something or get a helper to hold it.
- **Cut** - Simply cut along the fold with scissors. Do not work the scissors, but pull a little pressure against the inside of the fold to help maintain a straight cut and let the scissors glide through the plastic.

**Plastic Sheeting Cuts: First Roll** Figures 61, Two cuts:

- **The Roof Section** - One piece the full 10 foot width of the plastic sheeting and 14 feet long. Do not get confused with length and width of the plastic roll vs. the length and width of the greenhouse. The 10 foot length will cover the length of the greenhouse roof and the 14 foot section drapes over the roof from side to side.
- **The Sides** - Each is one piece the full 10 foot width of the plastic sheeting and 5½ feet wide. The 10 foot length will fit along the length of the greenhouse on each side.

**Second Roll** Figure 62, Nine cuts:

- **The Back** - Simple to cut. The single pieces is the full 10 foot width of the plastic sheeting and is cut 11 feet tall.
- **The Door** - cut 3½ x 8 feet (Door is covered in Step 12)
- **The Front Side Panels and Triangles** - Covered as one piece, so cut 4 feet wide and 7½ feet tall. The excess plastic of the triangle is removed later.

- **The Roof Strip** is a narrow 2 foot wide and 14 foot long piece that bridges the distance from the wooden roof section to the first pair of PVC Ribs. This is also how we cover the 10 foot long greenhouse with 10 foot wide roll of plastic. If you buy plastic sheeting in larger widths, the roof section could be made in one piece.
- **The Vent** - Covers the small triangular area above the door. Cut a 3 x 3 foot piece and then cut again along the diagonal to form a triangle.

**Table 4. Cut List for Plastic Sheeting (in Feet)**

| \  | Cuts for Plastic Sheeting | | |
|---|---|---|---|
| N | Section | Length | Width |
| 1 | Roof | 10 | 14 |
| 2 | Sides | 5½ | 10 |
| 1 | Back | 10 | 11 |
| 2 | Front Side Panel & Triangle | 7½ | 4 |
| 1 | Roof Vent (Cut Diagonal) | 3 | 3 |
| 1 | Door | 3½ | 8 |
| 1 | Roof Strip | 2 | 14 |

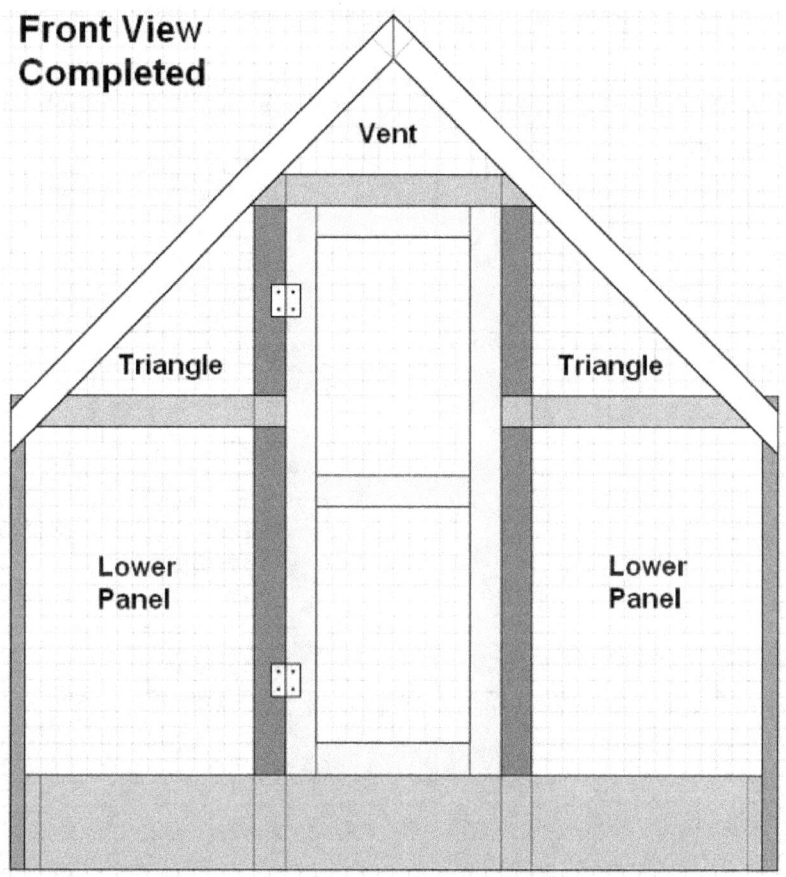

**Figure 60.** Labeled Front of Greenhouse Corresponds to Plastic Sheeting Cuts.

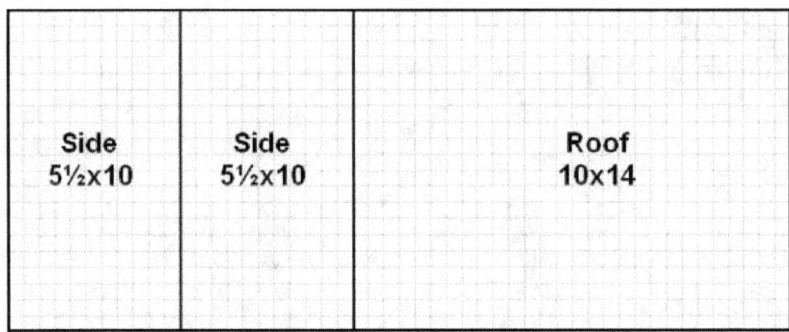

**Figure 61.** Cut Pattern for First Roll of Plastic Sheeting.

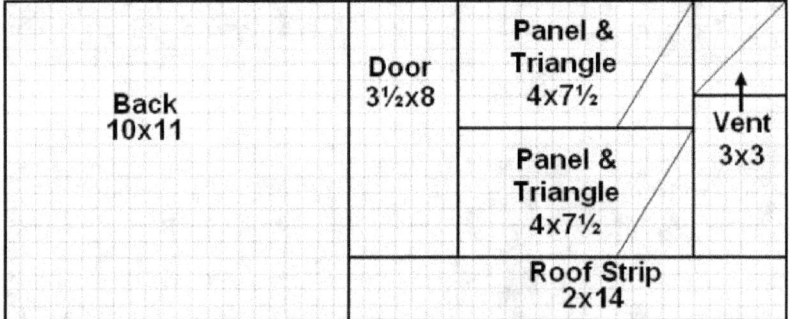

**Figure 62.** Cut Pattern for Second Roll of Plastic Sheeting.

**Step 11C: Clamp Plastic Sheeting to PVC Ribs** - The roof and roof strips are the only sections of plastic sheeting that are clamped to the PVC ribs with clamps. The plastic sheeting is clamped only to the outer pairs of PVC Ribs. The three center pairs of ribs support the plastic sheeting without any clamps.

The first rib supports, next to the wood roof section are attached and do not need to be removed for the entire growing season. The same clamps that hold the front end of the roof to the first ribs will also hold the back end of the roof strip when it is attached later.

The last pair of rib supports on the back end will hold both the back end of the roof section and the top of the back section when it is attached later.

The greenhouse will be ventilated by simply removing several of the top clamps and allowing the back end to open at the top. The clamps can be put back to hold the roof if it is windy. When the greenhouse is closed back up at night, simply re-attach the back flaps. Ventilation is very good with the front door open and the top of the back open at the same time.

**Attaching the Roof Section requires 4 tasks.**

- **1: Clamp one side of the 10x14 Roof Section** - Make sure the 10 foot length runs along the length of the side. The 14 foot length will cross over the top to the other side. Clamp temporarily with a spring clamp, or you can use the homemade clamps. The point is to hold the plastic in place, if you have enough helpers, you may not need clamps. This is a difficult task if it is windy.
- **2: Pull the other end over the top of the greenhouse and clamp** - Pass the 14 foot length of the roof section over the top of the greenhouse and temporarily clamp it to the opposite side.
- **3: Center the Roof Section** - Center the plastic sheeting in both directions so the same amount of extra plastic is at opposite ends. Depending on the length you cut the PVC ribs, the 14 foot length will have 6 - 12 inches of extra plastic on the sides and the 10 foot length will give about 6 inches at the first and last support ribs.
- **4: Attach The Roof Section** - To attach the plastic sheeting to the PVC ribs with clamps look at the images in Figure 63, Fig. 64 and Fig. 65. Using the finger savers is optional, but makes the job easier and protects the plastic sheeting. Attach at least 4 clamps on each side at the first and last rib as shown in Fig. 66. Also notice where the roof will be attached to the upper

frame with the furring strips, but this will be attached later.

**Figure 63.** Step 1- Attach Plastic Sheeting to PVC Frame with PVC Clamps. Position the homemade clamp and "finger savers" as shown in picture above. Begin spreading the clamp with the finger savers and push the plastic sheeting onto the PVC frame.

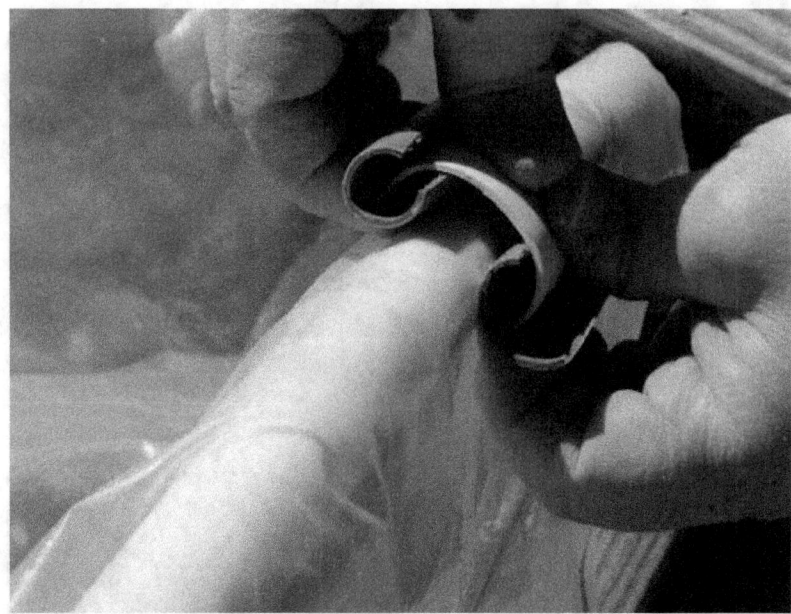

**Figure 64.** Step 2 - Attach Plastic Sheeting to PVC Frame with PVC Clamps. Half-way there, continue spreading and pressing toward the PVC frame.

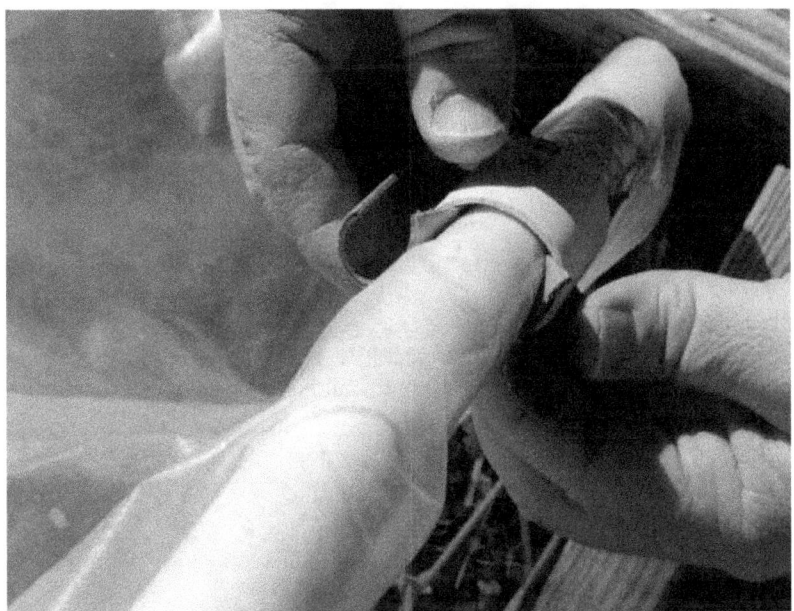

**Figure 65.** Step 3 - Attach Plastic Sheeting to PVC Frame with PVC Clamps. The clamp has been pushed onto the frame, now just pull out the finger savers.

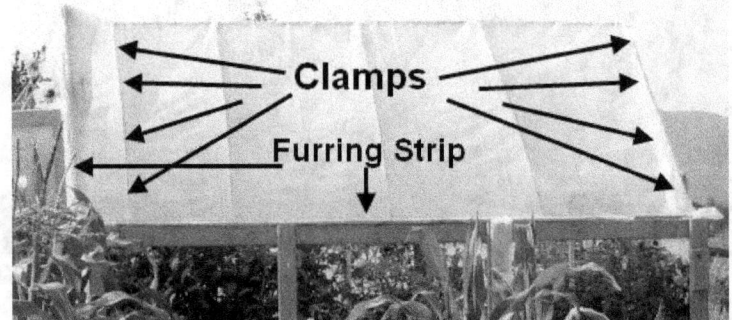

**Figure 66.** Placement of PVC Clamps on PVC Frame. Note: If using plastic sheeting larger than 10 feet wide, the roof would only be attached to the wooden roof section and the last pair of PVC ribs.

**Step 11D: Wrap Furring Strip with Plastic Sheeting and Attach to Frame** - All of the remaining sections of plastic sheeting are at least partially attached to the wood frame. All remaining sections of plastic sheeting except the roof strip and the door are attached to the base frame with a furring strip and are also either attached to the upper frame or the roof section with another furring strip. The four corners and the sides of the door frame are also secured with furring strips.

We start by wrapping (or rolling up) the furring strips that have been cut for each section with/in the plastic sheeting.

A 1x2 inch furring strip is really ¾ X 1½ inches. So to wrap around the furring strip once, it takes two ¾ inch sides plus two 1½ inch sides for a total of 4½ inches of plastic sheeting. To wrap the furring strip 1½ times it takes 6¾ inches and wrapping twice adds up to 9 inches.

Short sections are simple to wrap and attach without help. Longer sections are easier if you have a helper or you can use small strips of duct tape to hold the plastic in place to the furring strip before wrapping.

**To Wrap Furring Strips with Plastic Sheeting and Attach Plastic Sheeting to the Frame Requires 5 Tasks:**

- **Line Furring Strip up with Edge of Plastic Sheeting** - remember the sheeting is wider than the furring strip, so center the furring strip on the plastic.
- **Tape Plastic Sheeting to Furring Strips** - For all the long pieces; Sides, Back and sides of the roof, it helps to duct tape the plastic to the furring strip at several places, because these pieces are too long to hold only with your hands.
- **Roll Furring Strip up in Plastic Sheeting** - keep tension on the plastic, so the furring strip can be rolled tightly and evenly in the plastic. You may need to weigh down the opposite end to keep tension on the first side. Roll at least 1½ times. **Note:** This is a simple thing when attaching the first side of a plastic sheet, but it can be a little tricky when attaching the second side. The furring strip must be rolled in the plastic so the furring strip is perfectly flat with the frame and the plastic sheeting can not be too tight or too loose. This part may take two or three tries and adjustments to get it perfect.
- **Center Furring Strip** - if you centered the furring strip in the plastic before wrapping, simply center the furring strip so there is about equal space on each side of the gap that is being covered.

- **Attach Furring Strip to Frame** - Use 1½ inch screws and washers to secure the furring strip to the frame. Drive the screws in tight, but try not to drive them so tight that the washer cuts the plastic (Figure 67).

**Note:** It matters which way to roll the furring strip. Before attaching plastic to the greenhouse take a few moments to study the next few diagrams.

Figure 68 shows an example of how to attach plastic sheeting to the sides of the greenhouse. Both the lower and upper attachment of the furring strips to the upper and lower frame are shown in the same diagram; with lower attachment on the left and upper attachment on the right. Notice the plastic sheeting is aligned with the outside of both the upper and lower frames. In the diagram, the lower furring strip is rolled clockwise into the plastic and the upper furring strip is rolled counter-clockwise into the plastic.

Figure 69 is an example of how the roof strip is attached to the wooden roof section and also how the front panel and triangle sections were attached. In both cases, the furring strips were rolled counter-clockwise into the plastic.

Figure 70 shows how the single piece back section is attached to the upper frame in one piece, so the back section does not have to be cut. The furring strip was rolled clockwise into the uncut plastic which can be seen in the figure extending in two directions; down toward the base frame and up to be attached to the PVC frame.

**Figure 67.** Plastic Sheeting Attached to Frame with Furring Strip, Washers and Screws. Wrap the plastic several times around the furring strip and be careful not to cut the plastic.

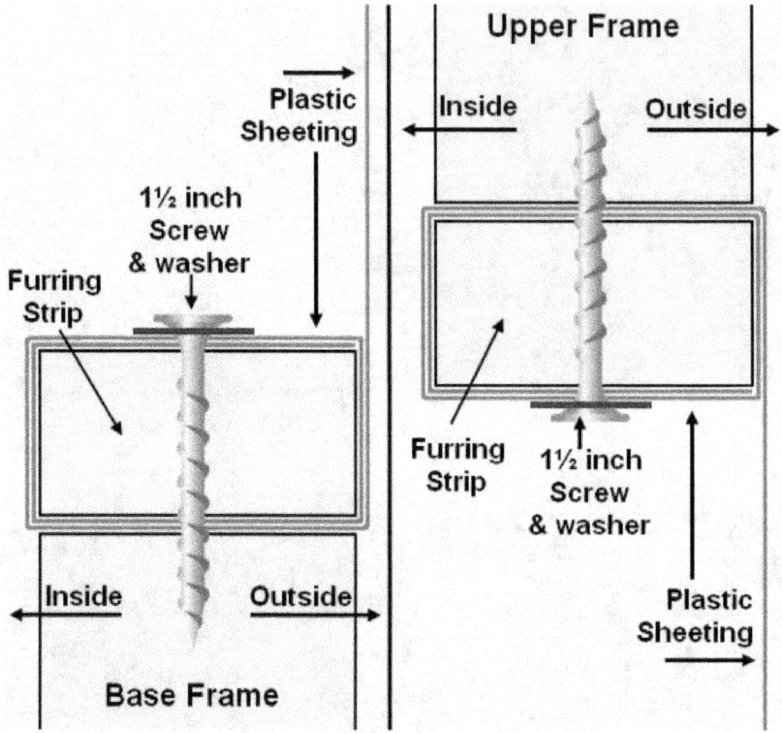

**Figure 68.** Plastic Sheeting Attachment to Upper Frame and Base Frame. The furring strips are attached on top of base frame and under upper frame. View diagram as if left side was on top of right side of diagram.

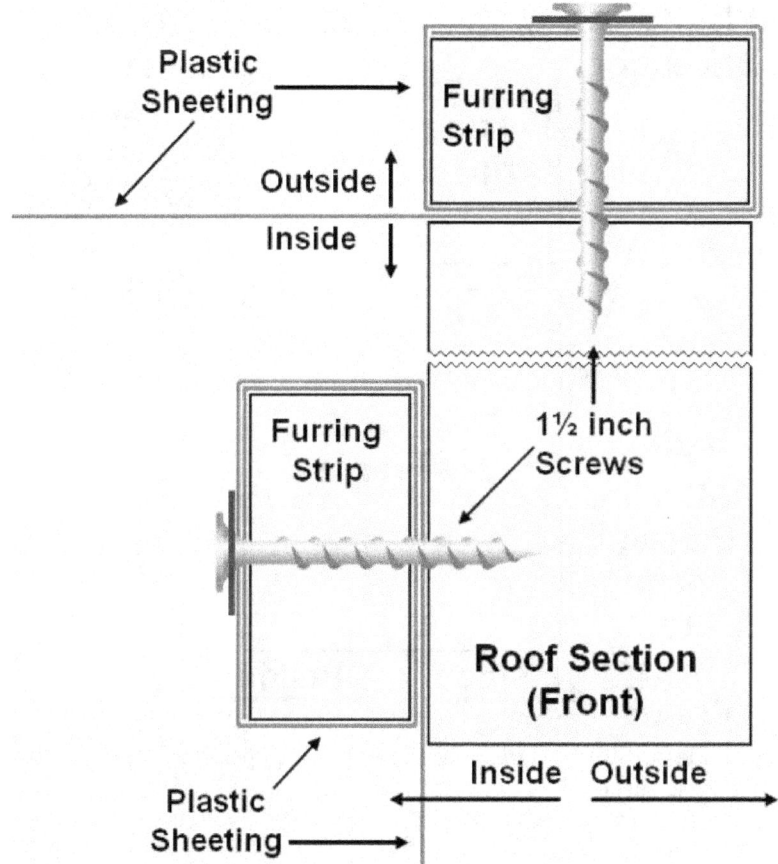

**Figure 69.** Plastic Sheeting Attached to Roof Section. Notice Roof Section attached on top and Front Panels attached on side or underneath.

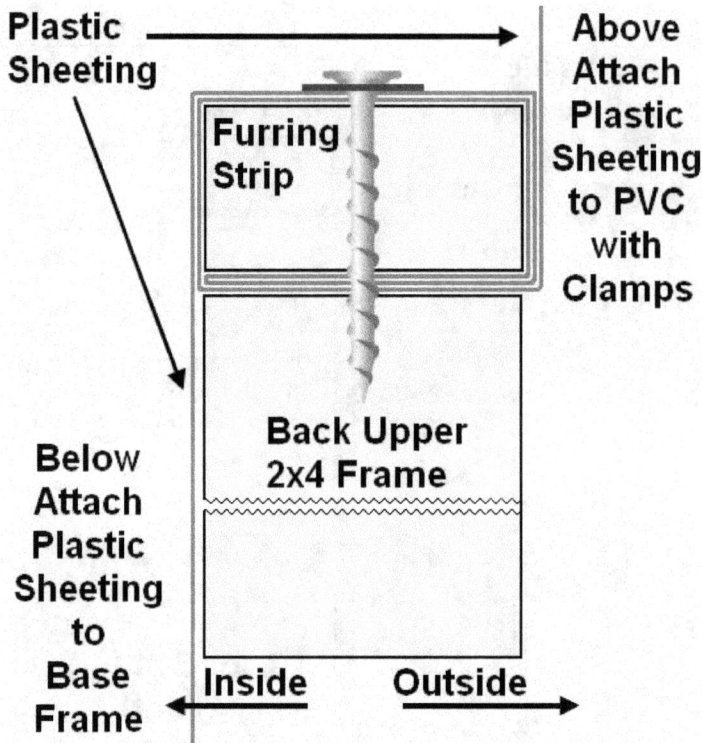

**Figure 70.** Plastic Sheeting Attachment to Back of Upper Frame. Wrap the uncut plastic at least twice around the furring strip.

**Directions for Attaching Each Section of Plastic Sheeting**

Continue covering the greenhouse by attaching the largest remaining sections first, which are the sides and the back. Each of these pieces are attached on top of the base frame at the bottom and are also attached to the upper frame. After the roof, I installed the back section first, but since the back is a little more complicated, I suggest you start with the side sections first.

**Attach Side Sections** - Attaching the first furring strip is simpler than attaching the second one, so I think it is easiest to start by attaching these pieces to the underside of the upper frame and then attaching the furring strips to the base frame.

- **Top** - Use uncut, 8 foot furring strips. Roll the 10 foot side of the plastic sheeting onto the furring strip as previously described and as shown in Figure 71. Attach with 1½ inch screws and washers underneath the upper frame as shown on the right side of Fig. 68.
- **Bottom** - Use uncut, 8 foot furring strips. Roll the opposite 10 foot side of the plastic sheeting onto the furring strip. Attach on top of the base frame as shown on the left side of Figure 68.
- **Ends** - Both ends of the side sections are attached to the corner vertical supports, but do not attach the ends until the front panels or the back sections are attached as shown in the next Step.

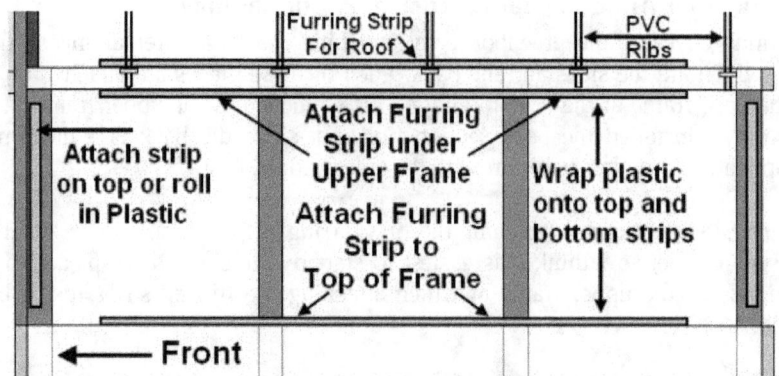

**Figure 71.** Placement of Furring Strips for Attachment of Plastic Sheeting to the Sides of the Greenhouse. Also refer to this figure for the placement of furring strips for securing the roof section to the upper frame sides.

**Attach Back Section** - the back section is a special case, since the back section is a single, uncut piece that is attached to the frame with a furring strip at the bottom, but attached to the PVC ribs with clamps at the top. This pieces also transitions from the inside of the frame at the bottom to the outside of the frame at the top and is also attached to the top of the upper frame with a furring strip. For this piece, you must start at the bottom and work up.

**Note:** The back piece has very little extra plastic to cover the space vertically. The 11 foot height leaves room to wrap the bottom furring strip with 6¾ inches of plastic and 9 inches to wrap the furring strip on the upper frame. If your PVC frame is 48 inches above the upper frame, that leaves 2¼ inches of overlap at the top. So do not use too much plastic at the bottom at the risk of running short at the top.

- **Bottom** - Use 92 inch furring strip. The back section is a 10 x 11 foot piece. More space is needed for the vertical distance, so roll the 10 foot side of the plastic sheeting onto the furring strip as shown in Figure 72 and Fig. 73. Attach on top of the base frame the same as the sides sections as shown on the left side of Fig. 68, but do not use more than 6¾ inches (wrap 1½ times).
- **Middle** - After the bottom of the back has been attached to the base frame, measure 9 inches on the plastic sheeting above the upper frame and tape the plastic at this point to the 1½ inch side of the furring strip. Roll into the uncut plastic sheeting (clock-wise), doubling the plastic as in Figure 70 until the 9 inches has been wrapped tight and the furring strip is flat against the top of the upper frame. Remember, the plastic sheeting transitions from the inside of the greenhouse to the outside at this point.
- **Top** - The upper part of the back section is attached to the PVC frame with homemade clamps. If you already attached the roof, then most of the clamps are holding the roof to the PVC frame. Starting at the lower clamps, remove the clamps one at a time from the roof section, pull the plastic from the back end up tightly and then clamp both the roof and back sections to the PVC frame at the same time. By leaving a small flap open at the top, we can create a very effective vent. I like to have a couple of extra clamps so I can open the flap, but do not have to put the clamps back to hold the roof.

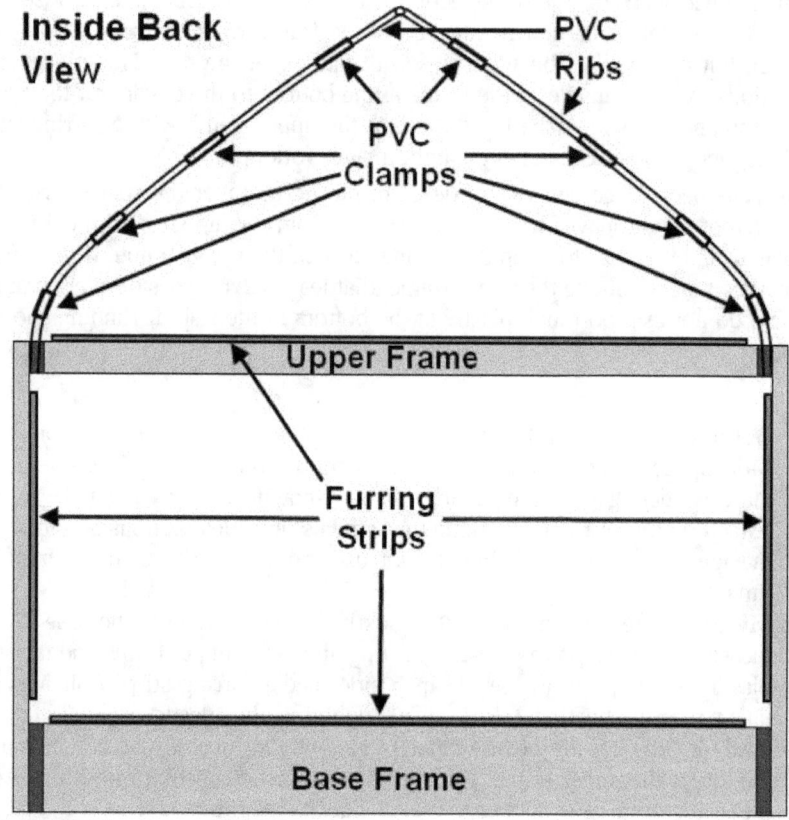

**Figure 72.** Placement of Furring Strips and Clamps for Attaching Plastic Sheeting to the Back of the Greenhouse.

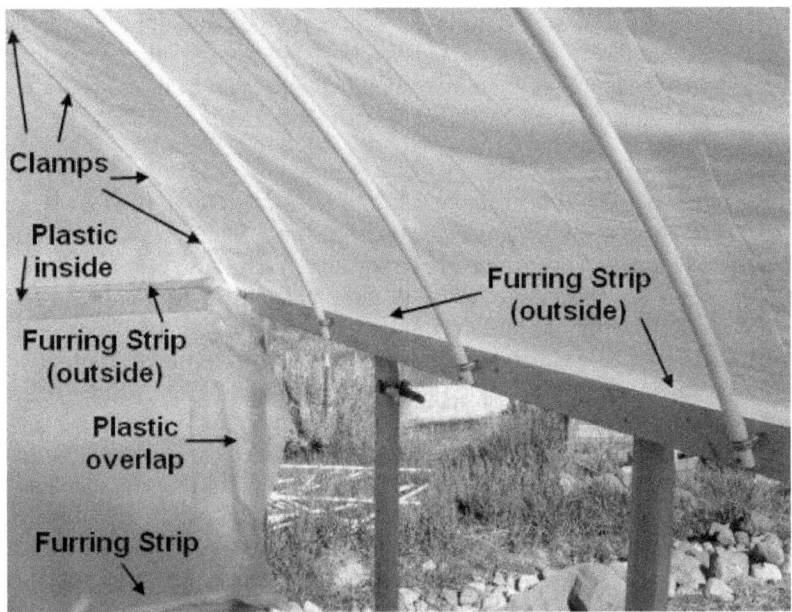

**Figure 73.** Placement of Furring Strips and Clamps for Attachment of Plastic Sheeting to the Back of the Greenhouse. Also refer to this figure for the placement of furring strips for securing the roof section to the upper frame sides.

**Attach Front Panels & Triangles** - The bottom of these front panels are attached just like the back and the sides were. Since these sections are attached to the 45° degree angle roof section, rolling the upper part of these sections are a little more complicated. I suggest starting with the bottom.

- **Bottom** - Use 24 inch furring strips and wrap them up in the four foot side of the plastic sheeting. Attach on top of the base frame as shown on the left side of Figure 68 with 3 screws and washers.
- **Top** - Pull the plastic upwards until tight and cut off the excess plastic in a 45° angle. Use the 30 inch furring strip and align it at a 45° degree angle and center as best you can. As you roll the plastic up, the furring strip will move down toward the angled roof section that the piece will be attached. Make sure to keep the plastic sheeting inside of the upper frame section. This is another place where it is difficult to get the furring strip to roll perfectly in the plastic. If it happens to roll up perfectly, you can attach to the underside of the roof section. If it does not, you can attach anywhere to the side of the roof section. It doesn't really matter, but Figure 69 shows the furring strip attached to the side of the roof section.
- **Ends** - The outer edges of the front panel and triangle sections are attached to the corner vertical supports and the inside edges are attached to the door frame. These are covered in the next Step.

**Attach Roof Strip** - The Roof strip is attached to the roof section with furring strips and is attached to the first pair of PVC ribs with the homemade clamps. The Roof section has to be attached with separate furring strips because of the roof angle, so wrapping the 14 foot piece of plastic onto these strips is a little awkward.

- **Roof Section** - Use 64 inch furring strips and wrap them up in the 14 foot side of the plastic sheeting. Easy to say, hard to do. A helper is useful for this task and it is probably best to wrap these strips on the ground and then transfer the wrapped furring strips to the top of the roof section. Place each furring strip on top of the plastic sheeting about 2-3 inches on each side of the center. The center of this 4-6 inch gap will sit on the roof peak. Attach the wrapped furring strips with washers and 1½ inch screws as shown in Figure 69.
- **First PVC Rib** - Remove the homemade clamps from roof that is already

attached to the PVC ribs and overlap the roof plastic and the roof strip plastic over the same PVC rib. Pull each in opposite directions and keep at tight as possible. Re-attach the homemade clamps over both layers of plastic sheeting to the PVC ribs with the clamps. You have already done this, but for reference, see the steps here: (Figure 63, Fig. 64 and Fig. 65).

**Attach Vent** - The vent section could be framed and attached with at small hinge to create a vent that could be easily opened and closed. The vent can also be permanently attached, because with the ability to open the back section and the door, there is plenty of ventilation. Last year, I attached the bottom of the triangle to the top of the door frame with a short furring strip, but temporarily attached the plastic sheeting of the vent to the roof section with spring clamps and opened and closed the vent by removing and replacing the clamps.

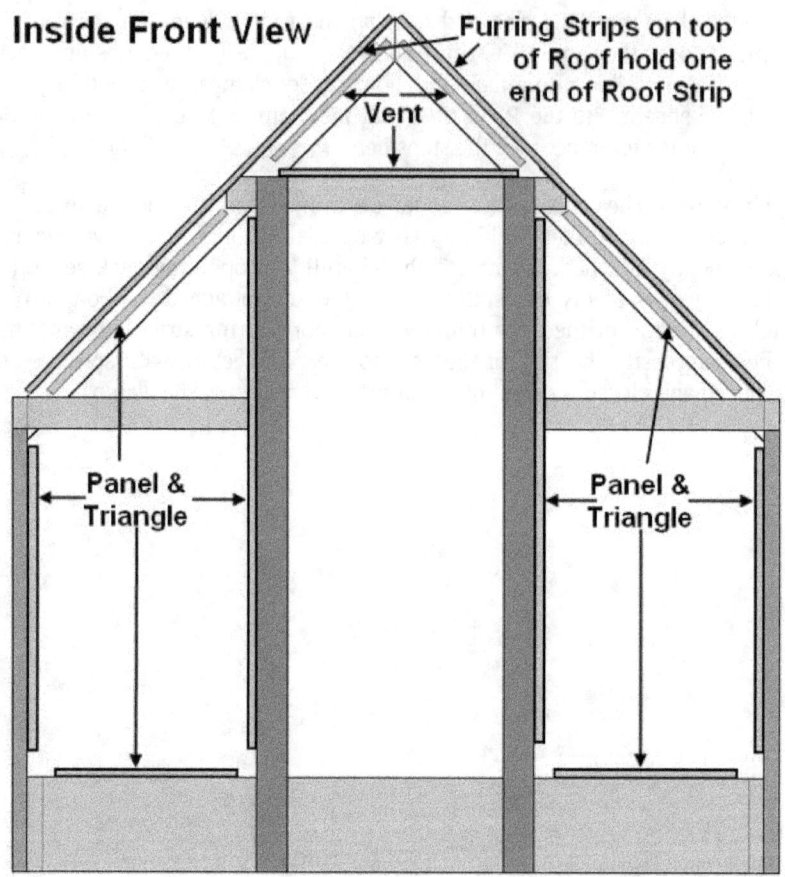

**Figure 74.** Placement of Furring Strips for Attachment of Plastic Sheeting to the Front of the Greenhouse. Attach on the inside.

**Step 11E: Secure Inside Corners and Sides of Door Frame** - In the corners, there is almost no overlap of plastic sheeting on the sides, but there should be at least 12 inches of overlap from the end piece in the back and almost 9 inches of overlap from the lower side panels.

**Secure Inside Corners:**

- From inside the greenhouse, overlap the extra plastic from the end piece or the side panels and press it against the corner vertical support with a 44 inch piece of furring strip. Center the furring strip so there is about equal space at the top and the bottom of the vertical support.
- Two options; 1-Roll or fold the furring strip up in the extra plastic sheeting until furring strip lays flat against the vertical support.
- Check to make sure there are no gapping holes between the plastic and the frame, especially at the top and bottom of the corners.
- Secure the plastic by driving four 1½ inch screws with washers through the furring strip into the vertical support.
- Do the same in the other three corners.

**Secure Door Frame:**

- Take a 68 inch furring strip and center it against the door frame with about equal space between the base frame and the top of the door frame.
- Roll the furring strip up in the extra plastic from the side panel that overlaps the door frame so the furring strip sits flat against the side of the door frame.
- Check to make sure there are no gapping holes between the plastic and the frame.
- Secure the plastic by driving 1½ inch screws with washers through the furring strip into door frame. Drive screws in the top and bottom, then space 4 other screws about every 16 inches.
- Do the same on the other side of the door.

**Step 11F: Seal Gaps** - Once the corners are sealed, except for the door, the Greenhouse should be fairly air tight. This is the time to double check around the corners and the seams to see if there are any gaps that need to be closed. None of the gaps should be more than a few inches. These can be closed with just a screw and washer or a short piece of scrap furring strip and a screw.

## Step 12: Build and Attach the Door

In my mind, it is the door that makes this a real greenhouse. This is a simple design, but works well. If you have a table saw or router and know how to make a lap joint, the door will be thinner and lighter. If you do not, not to worry.

Since the height of the door frame is 72 inches high, and the width is 28 inches (or whatever width you chose), the door needs to fit inside this space so it can swing freely. But we also want a tight fit to hold the heat in and keep cold air out. There are many ways to do this, but I chose to make it simple. I didn't use jams or casings, but feel free to do so if you like. I simply built the door 1/8 inch shorter than the door frame, giving 1/16 inch clearance all the way around.

Since the gaps in the door frame were filled and strengthened with 2x4 scraps, the door frame is a full 3 inches thick, which helps create a good seal against air flow. That seal against airflow is also increased if the furring strips are aligned along the edges of the door.

For those of you that choose to build the door by simply laying the cross pieces across the door sides, filling in the gaps of the door with scrap 2x4s will also make the door seal better.

**Steps to Building the Door**

[Step 12A: Mark and Cut Door Pieces](#)
[Step 12B: Cut Lap Joints](#)
[Step 12C: Pre-drill holes and Assemble Door](#)
[Step 12D: Cover Door with Plastic Sheeting](#)
[Step 12E: Attach Hinges and Mount Door](#)
[Step 12F: Seal Gaps](#)

**Step 12A: Mark and Cut Door Pieces** - If you have not already done so, mark and cut two 2x4 studs at 71 7/8 inches for the the door sides ([Table 2](#)) and the three cross braces according to the width of your door (Table 5) which is simply 1/8 inch shorter than the width of the door frame.

Table 5. Table Shows Cuts for Door Cross Braces for Various Door Sizes.

| Door Width | Cut Length | Lumber | | |
|---|---|---|---|---|
| | | 2x4 stud | 2x4 8-ft | 2x4 10-ft |
| 24 | 23 7/8 | 3 | | |
| 26 | 25 7/8 | 3 | | |
| 28 | 27 7/8 | 3 | | |
| 30 | 29 7/8 | 3 | | |
| 32 | 31 7/8 | | 3* | |
| 34 | 33 7/8 | | | 3# |
| 36 | 35 7/8 | | | 3# |

**\* If door width is 32 inches, must substitute 8-foot 2x4 for 2x4 stud.**
**#If door width is 34 or 36 inches, substitute 10-foot 2x4 for 2x4 stud.**

**Step 12B: Cut Lap Joints** - Lap joints (Figure 75)are hard to make by hand, so if you do not have a table saw or router or do not know how to make a lap joint , simply overlap the pieces just as we attached the Vertical Supports to the Upper Frame.

**Figure 75.** Lap Joints of Door. Lap joints are very strong and create a thinner door.

**Step 12C: Pre-drill holes and Assemble Door** - The assembly is basically the same whether using lap joints or simply attaching cross pieces on top of side pieces (Figure 76).

- **Clamp Pieces** - Clamp or hold pieces tightly together and flush and align all pieces.
- **Pre-drill Holes** - When satisfied the layout is correct, pre-drill at least three holes at all six joints.
- **Glue** - If you have wood glue, apply some to all joint surfaces.
- **Final Check for Alignment** - Re-clamp all pieces together and double check they are aligned correctly.
- **Start and Tighten Screws** - Attach all the joints with 1½ inch screws if using lap joints, otherwise use 3 inch screws.
- **Check Door Clearance** - Place door inside of door frame to make sure door has sufficient clearance. If the door binds anywhere with the door frame, the "high spots" will have to be filed or sanded until the door has clearance.

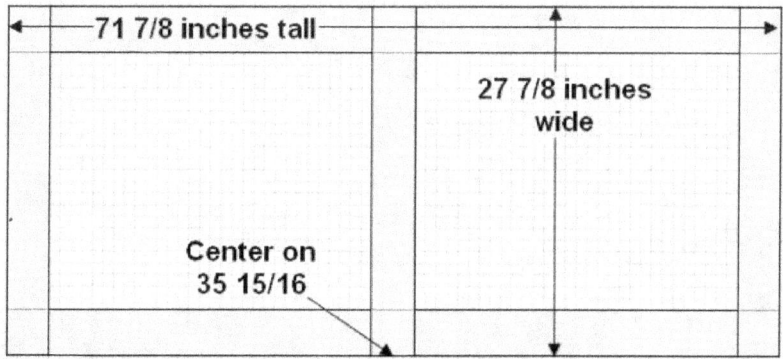

**Figure 76.** Diagram - Door Layout.

**Step 12D: Cover Door with Plastic Sheeting** - Covering the door with plastic sheeting is not much different than covering the other wooden parts of the greenhouse.

- Spread the plastic on the ground and center the door on top of it. The bottom side will become the inside of the door and the exposed frame will be the outside of the door.
- Pull the plastic tight in opposite directions and wrap/roll furring strips.
- Align and attach furring strips as show in Figure 77 and Fig. 78.

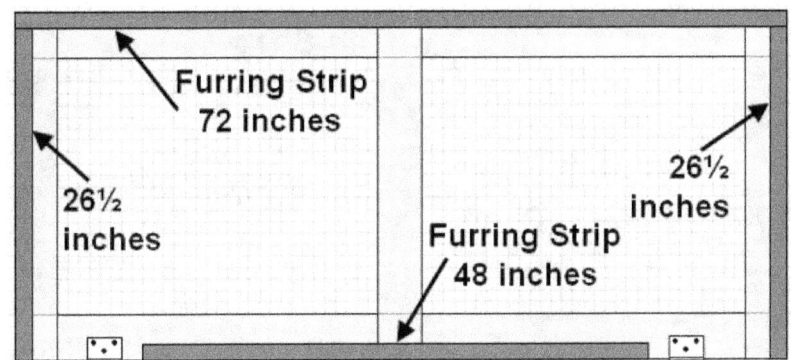

**Figure 77.** Furring Strip Placement to Cover Door with Plastic Sheeting.

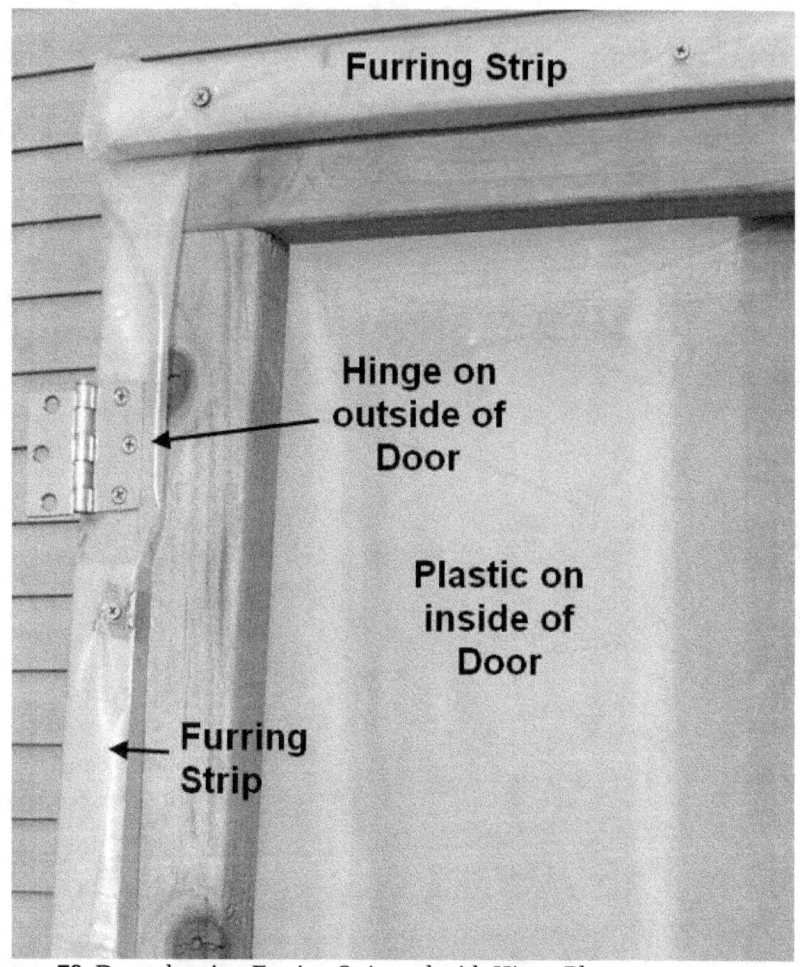

**Figure 78.** Door showing Furring Strip and with Hinge Placement.

**Step 12E: Attach Hinges and Mount Door** - Smooth finished side goes inside. Door opens to the outside, so you can always push the door open, but frame helps pull door open with handle. Feel free to add a handle, but it is not needed. Attach the hinges to the outside of the frame.

- Measure about 9 inches from the top and bottom of the door and align the hinge against the inside of door frame in the gaps between the furring strips.
- Attach the hinges with 1½ inch screws on top of the plastic sheeting.
- Place the door inside of door frame with hinges on the outside. The 6 mil plastic sheeting adds 0.006 inches per layer, but there should still be plenty of clearance.
- Shim the bottom of the door with anything (small nail, paper clip, match stick) about 1/16th inch thick to hold the door above the base frame.
- Align the hinge side of the door with the door frame and attach hinges with 3 inch screws.

**Step 12F: Seal Gaps** - Unless you plan on building the optional removable panels, the greenhouse is almost finished. All that remains is to seal any gaps around the door.

- Check the corners and edges where the furring strips do not reach to the edge. Any small gaps can be secured with a 1½ screw and washer, either alone or with small pieces of scrap furring strips can be use or patches made from folding several layers of duct tape.
- Also check around the door. To seal a gap above the door, I loosely folded 4 or 5 layers of scrap plastic sheeting and stapled it to the top of the door as shown in (Figure 79) to create a seal when the door is closed.

**Figure 79.** Roll or Folds of Plastic Sheeting to Seal Gap above Door.

### Step 13: Option: Build Removable Side Panels

Building the Removable Side Panels (Figure 80) adds and little more time and expense to the project, but we found it useful to be able to access plants from both sides, especially after the plants grew to almost fill the greenhouse. Removing the panels also helped cool the greenhouse on very hot days. I built 3 panels to fit between the Vertical Supports on the outside of the frame. I only placed panels on one side of the greenhouse. Remember, if you build panels for one side, you do not need to cover that side with plastic sheeting.

The removable panels fit between the Vertical Supports (35 1/3 inches) on the outside of the base and upper frames and span the 44½ inch distance between the base frame and upper frame. So panels are 48 x 35 5/16 (outside measure).

**Additional material:**

1. 6 - 2x2 lumber 8 foot (For 3 panels)
2. 5 - 8 foot 1x2 Furring strips
3. No additional Plastic Sheeting needed, cut three 60 x 48 inch pieces from the unused 5.5 x 10 foot side piece.
4. 8 - 6 inch bolts (3/8 or 1/4 inch), with 8 nuts and 8 wing nuts.
5. 8 - 2x4 blocks from scrap 6-10 inches

**Figure 80.** Optional Removable Panels.

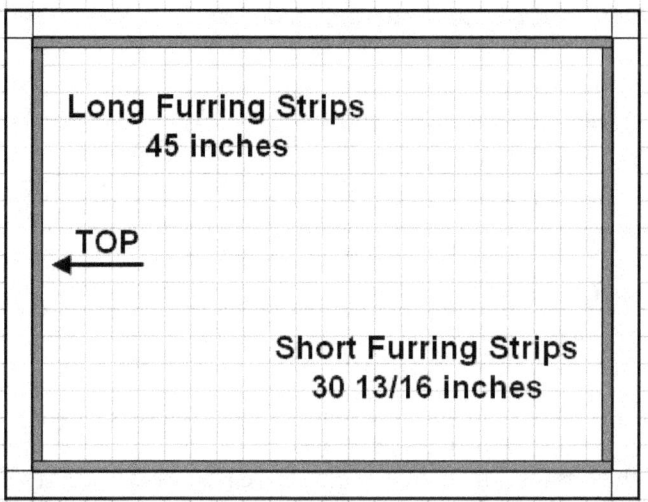

**Figure 81.** Furring Strip Placement to cover Removable Panel with Plastic Sheeting.

**Steps to Build and Attach Removable Side Panels** <u>1: Mark and Cut Panel Pieces</u>
<u>2: Cut Lap Joints</u>
<u>3: Pre-drill holes and Assemble Panels</u>
<u>4: Cover Panels with Plastic Sheeting</u>
<u>5: Attach Blocks to Greenhouse</u>
<u>6: Seal Gaps</u>

**1: Mark and Cut Panel Pieces -**
**If using lap joints:**

- Take three of the 8 foot 2x2s and cut 6 pieces 48 inches
- Take three of the 8 foot 2x2s and cut 6 pieces 35 5/16
- Take three of the 8 foot furring strips and cut 6 pieces 45 inches
- Take two of the 8 foot furring strips and cut 6 pieces 30 13/16 inches

**If using butt joints:**

- Take three of the 8 foot 2x2s and cut 6 pieces 48 inches
- Take three of the 8 foot 2x2s and cut 6 pieces 32 5/16
- Take three of the 8 foot furring strips and cut 6 pieces 45 inches
- Take two of the 8 foot furring strips and cut 6 pieces 30 13/16 inches

**2: Cut Lap Joints** -If you do not have a table saw or router or do not know how to make a lap joint (<u>Figure 75</u>), simply use butt joints as we attached the Base Frame (Example A; in <u>Figure 11</u>) The frames fastened with butt joints may be a little floppy, but should still work because the panels are clamped down tight against the greenhouse frame.

# 3: Pre-drill holes and Assemble Panel

- Clamp or hold pieces tightly together.
- When satisfied the layout is correct, for lap joints pre-drill at least two holes

at all four corners through lap joint. If using but joint, pre-drill at least two holes at all four corners through the sides of one 2x2 into the ends of the other.
- If you have wood glue, apply some to all joint surfaces.
- Re-clamp all pieces together and double check they are aligned correctly.
- Drive screws in to attach all the joints. If you made lap joints, use 1½ inch screws otherwise, for butt joints use 3½ inch screws.
- Place door inside of door frame to make sure door has sufficient clearance. If the door binds anywhere with the door frame, the "high spots" will have to be filed or sanded until the door has clearance.

## 4: Cover Panel with Plastic Sheeting

- Spread the plastic on the ground and center the panel on top of it. The bottom side will fit towards the inside of the greenhouse and the exposed frame will be on the outside.
- Pull the plastic tight in opposite directions and wrap/roll the 45 inch furring strips.
- Align and attach furring strips as show in Figure 81 using 1½ inch screws and washers.
- The 30 13/16 inch furring strips need to fit tight between the long furring strips. It is difficult to wrap and attach these strips. I have done it both ways; wrapping or not wrapping furring strips, but it works fine to simply press them into place on top of plastic sheeting and attach with 1½ inch screws and washers.

**5: Attach Blocks to Greenhouse** - The panels are held tight against the greenhouse with 2x4 blocks that are tightened down on bolts with wing nuts at the corners of each panel. The pairs of blocks on the two center panels hold the sides of two panels at the same time. The panels are easiest to place and remove if the blocks are perfectly centered on the Vertical Supports.

- Mark Vertical Supports for upper and lower blocks. The distance is not critical, but should be consistent (4-10 inches down from the upper frame and 4-10 inches up from the base frame).
- Find and mark the exact center of the Vertical Supports.

- Find and mark the exact center of the blocks. Find and mark the exact center in both directions for the blocks that will be used on the two center vertical supports.
- Drill holes (3/8 or 1/4 inch) in vertical support and blocks.
- Drill larger holes (½ inch) on outside of vertical support for nuts to be counter sunk in hole, so they are flush with wood. This is so the blocks are flush with the vertical supports
- Place bolt with head inside greenhouse, tighten with nut onto vertical support until flush
- Slide Block onto bolt and attach wing nut.
- With blocks oriented vertically, so they are out of the way, slide Removable panels in place between the vertical supports. Center the panels vertically and tighten wing nuts.

**6: Seal Gaps** - After attaching the removable panels to the greenhouse, check around all edges for gaps. I was able seal gaps by make "gaskets" by folding plastic sheeting and stapling it to the greenhouse frame (see Figure 80). Also notice roll of plastic sheeting added to the top of of the base frame that helps seal between the base frame and the removable panels.

# Section III: Results, FAQs, Notes, Info & Resources

### Results; A Work in Progress

After using our A-frame greenhouse for three seasons and the new 8x10 wood and PVC A-Frame greenhouse in 2012, we have had three very good crops of peppers and more tomatoes than we ever had. We also grew okra for the first time, proving that we can grow warm weather vegetable (Zones 7 & 8) in our cold (4a/4b) climate in our greenhouses.

The following pictures (Figures 82-89) are from our 2012 growing season and harvest.

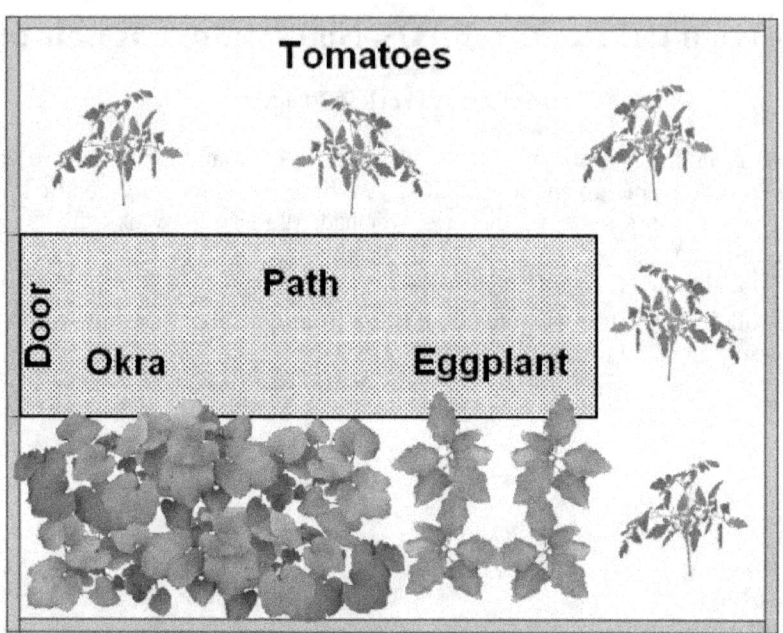

**Figure 82.** 2012 Greenhouse Plan. In 2012, we planted Tomatoes, Okra and Eggplant.

**Figure 83.** Young Okra 2012. Also shows Drip Line.

**Figure 84.** Maturing Okra in 2012.

**Figure 85.** Okra Harvest 2012.

**Figure 86.** Another Okra Harvest 2012.

**Figure 87.** Peppers Growing in the A-Frame Greenhouse 2012.

**Figure 88.** 2012 Poblano Pepper Harvest from a Single Plant.

**Figure 89.** 2012 Pepper Harvest from 5x10 A-Frame Greenhouse.

## Frequently Asked Questions

**Q: Your plan has 5 Ribs for 10 ft length. One on each end, one every 2½ feet. Would It be better to add an additional rib, so there is a rib every 2.0 feet?**

A: It obviously would not hurt to have an extra rib, but I haven't needed it. If you add the extra rib it will add the cost for two additional PVC pipes, two conduit straps and an extra zip-tie. If I were to build a true hoop house instead of an A-Frame, I would probably use the extra rib because snow would pile up on the flatter top. Snow does not accumulate very much on the A-frame.

**Q: How does the PVC A-frame hold up to the wind?**

A: The Greenhouse has withstood 70 mph wind gusts. Both sections; the PVC A-Frame held with home made PVC clamps and the wood frame with the permanently secured plastic had no problems.

Here is a video we took during a wind storm with no damage afterwards:

http://www.youtube.com/watch?v=kqyWdqICKqo

**Q: How many tomato plants can fit in the greenhouse?**

A: The 2012 floor plan for the greenhouse is shown in Figure 82.

**Q: What is the temperature difference between the inside and out side of the greenhouse?**

A: I took almost daily minimum and maximum temperatures inside both greenhouse in 2012 and compared to our min-max outside temperatures.

- During the first 14 days, the outside temperature was below 33° six times and below freezing four times, but was never below 34° inside either greenhouse.
- For those of you that pay attentions to Growing Degree Days (GDD - based on min 50° and max 90°), during an 84 day period (June 12-Sept 2), Outside = 1519 GDD; Greenhouse 1 = 1817 GDD; Greenhouse 2 = 1785 GDD.

**Q: What plants have you grown in the greenhouse?**

A: 2012 was our first season using the 8x10 foot walk-in greenhouse. We planted Tomatoes, eggplant and Okra. Tomatoes and Okra did extremely well.

The eggplants grew larger and healthier than any had outside of the greenhouse, but they never set any fruit. We suspect the extremely hot caused the flowers to drop. By the time fruit was setting, it was too late. But we did not grow any egg plants outside of the greenhouse, so we don't know if they would have set fruit and ripened or not.

In 2009-2012, we grew peppers in our smaller 5x10 A-Frame attached to the frames. We have successfully grown many varieties; Anaheim, Ancho/Pablano, many variety of Bell peppers, Cayenne, Corno di Toro, Fresno Chilies, Jalapeño, Serrano and even Habanera peppers. All have done extremely well except for the Habanera peppers.

## Q: Why do you use untreated wood and how long can we expect untreated wood to last?

See A Note about Using Pressure Treated Wood in Your Garden. All of our frames and the base frame for the greenhouse are built with untreated lumber. The oldest frames were built six years ago and starting to show a little weathering, but all of the wood is still very solid. Based on that fact, I expect they will last at least another 6 or 8 years.

## Q: How hard would it be to increase the length of your 10 foot greenhouse plan?

Not very hard at all. Material List provide in Table 6. Simply increase the length of the base and upper frame from 10 feet to the desired total length. You will also need one 20 foot PVC pipe that will be cut to length for the spine.

I would also add additional Vertical Supports for the frame and PVC Ribs for the A-Frame roof structure. Additional PVC ribs require additional Conduit Straps. There will be additional furring strips since there will be additional plastic. See Table x for the additional recommended 2x4x10, 2x2 studs, 1x2x8 furring strips and PVC pipe.

The most problematic item is the plastic sheeting, which normally comes in 10 foot widths. For greenhouse length larger than 10 feet, it would be much simpler to cut and more economical to buy UV treated plastic sheeting from an online greenhouse supply store in widths that more closely match the greenhouse length.

**Additional Vertical Supports** - The 4 Vertical Supports for the 10 ft length is plenty strong. That makes 3 spans (sections between supports) of 40 inches each and the frame should be sound as long as we don't exceed 40 inches between sections. For a safety margin, the span could be shortened as the frame becomes longer since the weight of the structure and the wind forces increase.

- For 12 ft, increase to 5 Vertical Supports (36 in. per span)
- For 14 ft, increase to 6 Vertical Supports (33.6 in. per span)
- For 16 ft, increase to 6 or 7 Vertical Supports (38.4 - 32 in. per span)
- For 20 ft, increase to 8 or 9 Vertical Supports (34.29 - 30 in. per span)

**Additional PVC Ribs** - The 5 Ribs for the 10 ft length is also plenty strong, and translates to 4 spans of 30 inches each. The roof should be strong as long as the span does not exceed 36 inches between rib supports.

- For 12 ft, keep at 5 or increase to 6 PVC Ribs (36 - 28.8 in. per span)
- For 14 ft, increase to 6 or 7 PVC Ribs (33.6 - 28 in. per span)
- For 16 ft, increase to 7 or 8 PVC Ribs (32 - 27.43 in. per span)
- For 20 ft, increase to 8 or 9 PVC Ribs (34.29 - 30 in. per span)

**Note:** Additional PVC clamps will be needed if the roof covering is two pieces instead of one.

**Table 6. Material List for Extended Lengths of the 8 Foot wide Wood and PVC A-Frame Greenhouse.**

| Material List for Extended Greenhouse Lengths | | | | |
|---|---|---|---|---|
| Material | 8x12 | 8x14 | 8x16 | 8x20 |
| 2 x 12 x 20 feet Lumber | | | | 2 |
| 2 x 12 x 16 feet Lumber | | | 2 | |
| 2 x 12 x 14 feet Lumber | | 2 | | |
| 2 x 12 x 12 feet Lumber | 2 | | | |
| 2 x 12 x 8 feet Lumber | 2 | 2 | 2 | 2 |
| 2 x 4 x 20 feet Lumber | | | | 2 |
| 2 x 4 x 16 feet Lumber | | | 2 | |
| 2 x 4 x 14 feet Lumber | | 2 | | |
| 2 x 4 x 12 feet Lumber | 2 | | | |
| 2 x 4 x 10 feet Lumber | 6 | 6 | 7 | 8 |
| 2 x 4 x 8 feet Lumber | 3 | 3 | 3 | 3 |
| 2 x 4 x 8 feet Stud | 6 | 8 | 6 | 6 |
| 1 x 2 x 8 feet Furring Strips | 14 | 15 | 16 | 18 |
| 3/4 inch PVC pipe 10 feet | 12 | 12 | 14 | 16 |
| 3/4 inch PVC pipe 20 feet | 1 | 1 | 1 | 1 |
| 1 inch EMT Metal Conduit Straps | 12 | 14 | 16 | 20 |
| #10 3.5 inch Exterior Screws | 1 lb | 1 lb | 2 lb | 2 lb |
| #10 3 inch Exterior Screws | 1 lb | 1 lb | 2 lb | 2 lb |
| #10 1.5 inch Exterior Screws | 1 lb | 1 lb | 2 lb | 2 lb |
| 2.5 inch zinc hinges | 2 | 2 | 2 | 2 |
| 6 mil Plastic Sheeting (10 x 25 feet) | 3 Roll | 3 Roll | 4 Roll | 4 Roll |
| 8 inch UV cable ties | 1 pk | 1 pk | 1 pk | 1 pk |
| PVC Clamps (home made) | 24 | 24 | 24 | 24 |

## Additional Notes about Using the Greenhouse

1. It can get very hot in a greenhouse. In 2011, we didn't ventilate the greenhouse soon enough on several occasions, allowing the temperature inside the greenhouse to get very hot (>130 degrees F). I was surprised, but this did not kill any of the plants, but we have to assume the plants were stressed. We also know that when temperatures climb above 85°F, tomatoes and other vegetables can fail to set fruit. When the outside temperature is above 85°F there is not much you can do except to shade the greenhouse and make sure the plants are not stressed for water. Many of our "full sun" vegetables suffer in hot temperatures. Partial afternoon shade can be a good thing. I plan to experiment more with afternoon shading on the hottest days.
2. We also don't always close the greenhouse early enough on some evenings and loose the opportunity to keep temperatures high during the evening and through the night (decreasing GDD).

3. We live in a dry climate where irrigation is a must inside or outside of the greenhouse. You may live in a wet climate, but once you cover greenhouse, you will have to water. We irrigate with drip lines that are attached to our secondary water system. I can water automatically with a timer or with a hose as needed. The drip system works very well and keeps the water on the soil under the mulch where it is needed. The drip line is stapled to the sides of the sides of the base frame and extends down and/or across each row as needed. The drip line can be seen in
Figure 83.

### Additional Information on Measuring, Marking and Cutting Lumber

If you don't have much experience marking and cutting lumber, practice on some scrap boards first until you learn how to mark exactly where you want the line, draw a straight line and then cut next to that line. If you are not careful, every board will be slightly long or short. If the sides or ends of the frame are not equal, the frame will never be square

Measure the board as accurately as possible and make a "pointed" mark on both edges of the board at the desired length (Figure 90). Use a framing square or a straight edge and draw a straight line between your marks (Figure 91). Start your cuts on the far side of that line (Figure 92). Remember that the saw blade removes material. Saw blades vary in thickness, but most remove between 1/8 to 1/16th of an inch of wood.

**Figure 90.** Measure and Mark Lumber. Mark Board on Both Sides with a Point exactly where Cut should be.

**Figure 91.** Mark Cut Line. Use Framing Square or other Straight Edge.

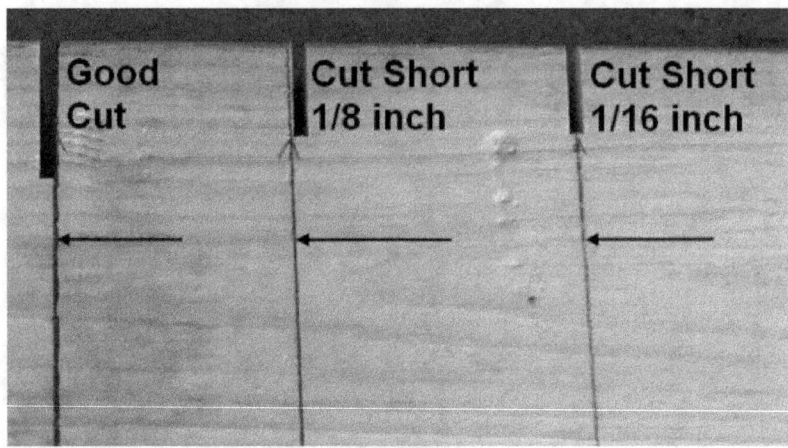

**Figure 92.** Picture showing Good and Bad Cuts.

In Figure 92 above, the cut on the far left is a good cut assuming I measured from right to left. The cut just shaved the thin pencil line. If you are using a fat pencil mark, cut so you remove half of the line. Professional carpenters mark a large "X" on the side of the line that represents the piece to be cut to make sure they cut on the other side of the line.

The Center cut is about an 1/8 inch short, because I cut on the wrong side of the line and my saw blade is about 1/8th inch thick.

The Cut on the far right is about 1/16 inch short because I cut down the center of the line.

## A Note about Using Pressure Treated Wood in Your Garden

Chances are, you have seen this information before, but if not, take a minute to read.

Note that I suggest using untreated lumber for your frames. There have been concerns that the chemicals used to treat the wood may get into the vegetables. I read recently that Arsenic can be taken up by plants, but only if the soil is deficient with Phosphorus. One thing I have learned is that you can never say never for Biology. It appears that the EPA doesn't want us to even touch arsenate treated wood. Since the EPA banned the sale of lumber treated with chromated copper arsenate (CCA) for residential use in 2003 (12/31/2003), the EPA recognizes several alternatives:

- Alkaline Copper Quaternary (ACQ)
- Copper Azole (CA)
- Micronized Copper Quaternary (MCQ)

I have seen in some of the gardening forums that the new treated wood products are safe to use for raised garden bed frames, but needed to do the research for myself.

For Alkaline Copper Quaternary (ACQ), the Copper is the primary active ingredient and is described as being similar to chemicals used to keep swimming pools clean and primarily prevents fungal growth. The Quat formulation is similar to other bio-degradable cleaners and preservatives and is a back up for Copper resistant fungi and termites. There are no EPA listed carcinogens in ACQ. Research has not identified any direct threats to humans, but the products do leach copper, which is very toxic in aquatic systems. Brand Names include YellaWood, Preserve® and NatureWood®.

For Copper Azole (CA), as with ACQ, the Copper is the primary ingredient (98%) and the tebuconazole fungicide is the backup (<1%). Brand names are Wolmanized, Tanalith®, or Tanalised® and Residential Outdoor®.

Micronized Copper Quaternary (MCQ), is the same chemical formula as ACQ, but it is first ground into tiny particles (micron sized) then are injected into the cellular structure of the wood under high pressure. This process releases 90-99% less copper into the environment, which is good news for aquatic environments. MicroPro claims that the small amount of Copper that is released, binds quickly to organic compounds in the soil, making it biologically inactive. The MCQ treated wood does not show as much color change as the other treatment processes. It is also not as corrosive to fasteners as ACQ or CA treated wood, but you would still need to use approved fasteners. because less corrosive does not mean non-corrosive. Brand names for MCQ treated wood include Yellawood MCQ, MicroPro® and SmartSense®.

Since the new wood preservatives use Copper, treated wood is more likely to react and corrode standard nails, screws and other fasteners. Building codes have begun to require stainless steel, ceramic coated or hot dipped galvanized fasteners to prevent failures due to corrosion when using the ACQ, CA or MCQ treated wood products. Another consideration with treated wood is the fact that the treatment process also pumps water back into the dry wood as it applies the chemical treatment. Since the wood may still have a high moisture content it may shrink, warp and split as it dries out.

We are always cautioned to wear gloves, dust masks and eye protection when handling and cutting both treated and untreated wood. We are also advised to wash our hands after handling the new types of treated lumber, to wash clothes separately and are warned not to burn treated lumber or use it as mulch.

Another consideration with treated wood is the fact that the treatment process also pumps water back into the dry wood as it applies the chemical treatment. Since the wood may still have a high moisture content it may shrink, warp and split as it dries out.

Am I convinced that it is safe to use the new copper treated wood products for raised garden beds? Yes, it is safe for people, but it is not safe for aquatic systems. The new Micronized process is better and leaches 90% less copper back into the environment than the CA or ACQ methods.

## Using Untreated Wood

As I write this, our untreated wood frames have been in the soil for between 3 and 6 years now. Yes, they have weathered and yes, there are some signs of decay to the wood that is underground, but they are still sound and solid and I expect to get another 4 or 5 years before I have to replace them. The same cold, dry climate that make it hard for me to grow vegetables also slows the decomposition rate of untreated wood. Untreated wood may not last as long in your climate. If I had to choose, I would use the Micronized Copper Quaternary (MCQ) treated wood. While leaching any Copper into the soil is not good, leaching 90% less would be better.

I read recently that organic farmers could not declared their produce "Organic" if they had treated lumber that contacted their soils or animals. I did a little research and found the statues (see § 205.206 & § 205.602 below*) that regulate the use of treated wood under the Organic Food Production Act. The actual language in § 205.206 refers only to arsenate materials in new and replacement installations, not to existing installations. After further research, it appears that existing installations that use even arsenic based PT wood are "grandfathered". So it is still possible for certified Organic Vegetables to be produced in raised beds constructed from arsenate treated wood if they received their certification prior to the last day of 2003.

*§ 205.206: Crop pest, weed, and disease management practice standard. (f) The producer must not use lumber treated with arsenate or other prohibited materials for new installations or replacement purposes in contact with soil or livestock.

*§ 205.602: Nonsynthetic substances prohibited for use in organic crop production. The following nonsynthetic substances may not be used in organic crop production: (b) Arsenic.

## PVC Pros, Cons & Info And PVC Safety Precautions

### Pros of using PVC pipe

- Cheap
- Easy to find
- Light weight
- Easy to work with (cut, bend, drill, glue)
- Can also provide irrigation
- Connect permanently or temporarily
- Does not degrade significantly in sunlight
- Cast very little shade into the greenhouse

## Cons of using PVC pipe

- A petrol-chemical product that produces hazardous waste by-products and pollutants; including PCBs, chlorinated dioxins and furans, hexachlorobenzene, octachlorostyrene and phthalates.
- PVC is not bio-degradable or recyclable.
- There have been some concerns about PVC pipes manufactured prior to 1977 for drinking water - Make sure to use PVC pipe that is marked with NSF-PW or NSF-61.
- Cutting PVC pipe creates electro-statically charged dust that sticks to everything.

**Precautions about Using PVC Pipe** As with other plastic products, there have been some questions raised recently about the safety of drinking water from PVC pipes, especially PVC pipes manufactured prior to 1977. We should probably be more concerned about drinking water from the garden hose than using PVC pipe for structural support for a greenhouse, but perhaps it is wise to err on the side of caution.

- This plan uses PVC pipe only as structural support for the greenhouse.
- Use only PVC pipe that is marked with NSF-PW or NSF-61, which the EPA claims is safe for drinking.
- We are not convinced PVC is safe to use as a growing container.
- Take precautions not to inhale the PVC dust when cutting PVC pipe. A PVC pipe cutter does not make dust, but sawing PVC pipe creates a lot of fine electrostatic dust (really more like tiny chips or granules). The PVC dust/chips/grains stick to everything. Be careful about taking the dust into the house or around children.

**Other PVC Information**

I have read claims that PVC pipe deteriorates in the sunlight. I have not found that to be the case. In fact, I found a study that tested PVC Pipe after 15 years exposed to sunlight. Sunlight will effect the PVC, but according to the study (see UNI-TR-5) by Unibell.org, only the outer 0.002 inches was visibly effected after 15 years and the pipe passed all standard requirement tests. All UV deterioration can be stopped if the PVC pipe is painted (acrylic or latex paint) or covered with tape.

## Notes about Plastic Sheeting

**Plastic Coverings** - Choosing the Right Greenhouse film AKA agricultural plastic, poly-film and greenhouse plastic.

As I have learned, all Plastic Coverings are not created equal. There are several options for buying plastic sheeting to cover the greenhouse:

- **Utility Grade** (6 mil) polyethylene plastic (PE)
- **UV protection** - Protects plastic film from Sunlight - should last 4 years
- **Thermal protection** - Reflects IR back into greenhouse - claims to cut heating costs 15-30% and to maintain higher temperatures at night if you don't heat the greenhouse
- **Anti condensation** - condensation attached to film can reduce sunlight and reduces dripping onto plants.

I have used the 6 mil (utility grade) polyethylene plastic sheeting (Figure 93) readily available at most home improvement and hardware stores, but can only use it for one season. The plastic sheeting is still good at the end of the season, but I tried to reuse some of the plastic for a second season and it became very brittle and began to disintegrate. After it disintegrated, it was nearly impossible to pick up. So if using plastic sheeting without UV protection, only use it for one growing season.

Plastic sheeting specifically designed for use on greenhouses are also available that have UV protection and are supposed to last 4 years or more. It could be cheaper in the long run to buy UV protected plastic sheeting even with the increased costs and shipping charges.

UV plastic may be able to stand up to the sun, but there seem to be issues with the UV treated plastic deteriorating. Some say it is the chlorine gas that escapes from new PVC pipe. Other sources say it is the heating and cooling effect on the plastic that occurs most along the support ribs and spine. I think it may also be rubbing between the plastic sheeting and any supports (wood or PVC) caused by the wind.

My PVC pipe has been weathering for at least 3 and 4 years, so maybe I won't have any more issues with off-gassing of chlorine, but I have never noticed any deterioration issues of the plastic sheeting next to PVC pipe even when it was new.

It has been recommended that PVC pipes be painted or taped or wrapped to prevent contact between the plastic and the PVC, and I have seen where the warranty for UV protected plastic sheeting may be void if placed over PVC pipe, but I have not noticed any problems from plastic sheeting contacting PVC pipes.

I only use the plastic sheeting for one year, but in four years of using the utility grade polyethylene to cover PVC pipe, I have only seen a few small holes. For a temporary fix, I simply cover the hole with a small piece of clear packing tape. I have not had any problems when I started with new plastic each Spring.

The plastic sheeting and the home made clamps have survived wind storms of more than 50 mph.

I intend to try the UV plastic because I don't like the fact that I throw away plastic sheeting every year. I have not yet done so because I can't justify the extra cost for UV protected Plastic. I have no doubt the UV protected sheeting will survive the Sunlight, I do question if it can survive the wind and snow for four years. If it could not, the extra money would be wasted. If I took the UV plastic down every winter, it may last for many years.

**Figure 93.** Example of Utility Grade (6 mil) Plastic Sheeting. This plastic can only be used to cover the greenhouse for a single season.

## Additional Methods for Attaching Plastic Sheeting to the Greenhouse

- Weight down plastic sheeting on side with lumber, cinder blocks, rocks, gravel or soil
- Attach plastic sheeting to bed frame with spring clamps
- Make a loop from the plastic sheeting by sandwiching plastic between wooden furring strips and insert wood or rebar for weight
- Commercially available channel and "wiggle wire"
- Screw homemade PVC channel to frame, snap into place with PVC Pipe
- Reinforce plastic sheeting with Mesh tape and attach with zip-ties Staple plastic sheeting with batten material (strong flexible rubber-like material like agricultural drip-line)

**Additional Greenhouse Covering Materials** There are a variety of materials that can be used to cover a greenhouse today. With the current explosion of interest from both commercial farmers and backyard gardeners, the options for materials are constantly expanding. Greenhouse covering material ranked (high to low) by estimated cost to cover an 8x10 foot greenhouse:

- **Glass** - $1,340-$2,880 (3/16 -1/4 inch; annealed or tempered glass)
- **Polycarbonate** (rigid panels or flexible rolls) - $1,280 (16mm triple wall panels)
- **Acrylic** (rigid panels) - $1,150 - $1,210 (twin acrylic panels)
- **Fiberglass** (rigid panels or flexible rolls) - $800 (rigid panels)
- **Polyethylene Panels** (semi rigid panels or flexible rolls) - $510 -$675 (3 - 5 mm flexible panels)
- **Vinyl** - $280 (Walls only, roof would still have to be covered with another material)
- **UV treated Polyethylene Plastic Sheeting** - $100 (6 mil, 4 years)
- **Polyethylene Plastic Sheeting** - $50 (6 mil, 1 year utility plastic)

For more info and sources for greenhouse covering materials, Read our post here.

## Resources

Click on links for additional information.

USDA Plant Hardiness Zone Map - Determine which plants are most likely to thrive at a location

NOAA Regional Climate Centers - For frostfree dates by region: Western, High Plains, Souther, Midwestern, Northeast & Southeast.

NOAA Freeze/Frost Maps - Spring & Fall Freeze Occurrence Maps (10% Probability), Freeze Free Period Map (90% Probability)

Greenhouse Tips - Additional information and tips about building greenhouses and gardening from the author's blog, HomemadeHints.com.

Contact Us - We value reader feedback. If you have comments, questions or see errors in this book, please feel free to contact us. Unfortunately, every device displays a little differently (optimally viewed on a larger computer screen with free Kindle reading apps) so it is difficult to make everything perfect for every device, but if you see sections or photos not displaying correctly, please let us know.

You can also Find Us on Facebook. Feel free to post any of your questions on our wall.

# Section IV: List of Figures and Tables

## List of Figures

- Fig. 1. Picture - The Wood and PVC A-Frame Greenhouse Early 2012 Growing Season
- Fig. 2. Picture - The Wood and PVC A-Frame Greenhouse Late 2012 Growing Season
- Fig. 3. Picture - Our Raised Beds and Both Greenhouses Late 2012 Growing Season
- Fig. 4. Picture - Front View of Both Greenhouses
- Fig. 5. Picture - Our Raised Garden Beds Showing Future Site of the New Greenhouse
- Fig. 6. Diagram - Example of Building Site with a Mild Slope
- Fig. 7. Diagram - Example of Building Site with a Steep Slope
- Fig. 8. Diagram - Example of Building Site Showing Excavation of a Steep Slope
- Fig. 9. Diagram - Example of Slope at My Building Site
- Fig. 10. Diagram - Example of Slope at My Building Site Showing Stones For Support
- Fig. 11. Diagram - Three Different Ways to Connect an 8 x 10 ft Frame
- Fig. 12. Picture - Marking Holes to be Pre-Drilled
- Fig. 13. Picture - Use Long Screws for a Strong Frame
- Fig. 14. Picture - Drill Pilot Holes
- Fig. 15. Picture - Start Screws
- Fig. 16. Picture - Hold Frame Firmly while Driving Screws
- Fig. 17. Picture - Finished Base Frame
- Fig. 18. Diagram - Scale Drawing of 10 ft X 8 ft Bed Frame
- Fig. 19. Picture - Leveling the Base Frame I
- Fig. 20. Picture - Leveling the Base Frame II
- Fig. 21. Picture - The Base Frame is Level
- Fig. 22. Picture - Large Rocks Used to Support the Hanging End of My Base Frame
- Fig. 23. Diagram - Base Frame Layout
- Fig. 24. Picture - Nearly Completed Wood and PVC A-Frame Greenhouse
- Fig. 25. Diagram - Front View of Greenhouse Frame
- Fig. 26. Diagram - Side View of Greenhouse Frame

- Fig. 27. Diagram - Left Front/Right Rear Base Frame Corner showing Attachment of Vertical Support
- Fig. 28. Picture - Left Rear/Right Front Base Frame Corner showing Attachment of Vertical Support
- Fig. 29. Picture - Left Front/Right Rear Corner of Upper Frame
- Fig. 30. Diagram - Side View - Attachment of Remaining (non-corner) Vertical Supports
- Fig. 31. Diagram - Top View of Left Front/Right Rear Corner of Base Frame
- Fig. 32. Diagram - Top View - Left Front/Right Rear of Upper Frame Corner Attachment to Vertical Support
- Fig. 33. Diagram - End View of Right Front/Left Rear Corner of Upper Frame Attachment to Vertical Support
- Fig. 34. Picture - Top View of Finished Left Front/Right Rear Corner of Upper Frame
- Fig. 35. Diagram - Top View of Finished Left Front/Right Rear Corner of Upper Frame
- Fig. 36. Diagram - End View of Finished Right Front/Left Rear Corner of Upper Frame
- Fig. 37. Diagram - Front View of Door Frame
- Fig. 38. Diagram - Side View of Door Frame
- Fig. 39. Diagram - Front View of Top of Door Frame
- Fig. 40. Diagram - Front View of Attached Roof Section
- Fig. 41. Picture - Front View of 45° Roof Peak
- Fig. 42. Picture - Rear View of Roof Peak
- Fig. 43. Diagram - Step 1 of Alternate Method for Constructing 45° Roof Peak
- Fig. 44. Diagram - Step 2 of Alternate Method for Constructing 45° Angle Peak
- Fig. 45. Diagram - Side View of Door Frame and Roof Section
- Fig. 46. Diagram - Front View showing Gaps to be Filled to Stiffen and Flush Door Frame
- Fig. 47. Diagram - Side View of Gaps in Door Frame Filled to Stiffen and Flush the Door Frame
- Fig. 48. Picture - Gaps Filled in Door Frame
- Fig. 49. Diagram - Front View - Cut-away of Frame Section from Door Frame and Trimmed Door Frame
- Fig. 50. Picture - Conduit Strap in Back Corner of Upper Frame
- Fig. 51. Picture - Drill Holes at an Angle in the Top of Each PVC Rib
- Fig. 52. Diagram - Comparing PVC A-Frame, Ellipse and Straight Line
- Fig. 53. Picture - Loosely Attach Zip-ties Between Opposing PVC Ribs

- Fig. 54. Picture - Slide the Single Uncut 10 foot PVC Pipe (Spine) in between all Zip-ties
- Fig. 55. Picture - PVC Roof Support Ribs Attached to Upper Frame
- Fig. 56. Picture - Slowly Tighten all Zip-ties
- Fig. 57. Picture - Final Configuration of PVC Spine and Support Ribs
- Fig. 58. Picture - Homemade PVC Clamps
- Fig. 59. Picture - Homemade "Finger Savers"
- Fig. 60. Diagram - Labeled Front of Greenhouse Corresponds to Plastic Sheeting Cuts
- Fig. 61. Diagram - Cut Pattern for First Roll of Plastic Sheeting
- Fig. 62. Diagram - Cut Pattern for Second Roll of Plastic Sheeting
- Fig. 63. Picture - Step 1 Attach Plastic Sheeting to PVC Frame with PVC Clamps
- Fig. 64. Picture - Step 2 Attach Plastic Sheeting to PVC Frame with PVC Clamps
- Fig. 65. Picture - Step 3 Attach Plastic Sheeting to PVC Frame with PVC Clamps
- Fig. 66. Picture - Placement of PVC Clamps on PVC Frame
- Fig. 67. Picture - Plastic Sheeting Attached to Frame with Furring Strip, Washers and Screws
- Fig. 68. Diagram - Plastic Sheeting Attachment to Upper Frame and Base Frame
- Fig. 69. Diagram - Plastic Sheeting Attachment to Roof Section
- Fig. 70. Diagram - Plastic Sheeting Attachment to Back of Upper Frame
- Fig. 71. Diagram - Placement of Furring Strips for Attachment of Plastic Sheeting to the Sides of the Greenhouse
- Fig. 72. Diagram - Placement of Furring Strips for Attachment of Plastic Sheeting to the Back of the Greenhouse
- Fig. 73. Picture - Placement of Furring Strips and Clamps for Attachment of Plastic Sheeting to the Back of the Greenhouse
- Fig. 74. Diagram - Placement of Furring Strips for Attachment of Plastic Sheeting to the Front of the Greenhouse
- Fig. 75. Picture - Lap Joints of Door
- Fig. 76. Diagram - Door Crosspiece Layout
- Fig. 77. Diagram - Furring Strip Placement to Cover Door with Plastic Sheeting
- Fig. 78. Diagram - Door showing Furring Strip and Hinge Placement
- Fig. 79. Picture - Roll or Folds of Plastic Sheeting to Seal Gap above Door
- Fig. 80. Picture - Optional Removable Panels

- Fig. 81. Diagram - Furring Strip Placement to cover Removable Panel with Plastic Sheeting
- Fig. 82. Diagram - 2012 Greenhouse Plan
- Fig. 83. Picture - Young Okra 2012
- Fig. 84. Picture - Maturing Okra 2012
- Fig. 85. Picture - Okra Harvest 2012
- Fig. 86. Picture - Another Okra Harvest 2012
- Fig. 87. Picture - Peppers Growing in A-Frame Greenhouse 2012
- Fig. 88. Picture - 2012 Poblano Pepper Harvest from Single Plant
- Fig. 89. Picture - 2012 Pepper Harvest from 5x10 A-frame Greenhouse
- Fig. 90. Picture - Measure and Mark Lumber
- Fig. 91. Picture - Mark Cut Line
- Fig. 92. Picture - Showing Good & Bad Cuts
- Fig. 93. Picture - Example of Utility Grade Plastic Sheeting

# List of Tables

- Table 1. Material List for 8x10 Wood and PVC A-Frame Greenhouse
- Table 2. Cut List for 8x10 Wood and PVC A-Frame Greenhouse
- Table 3. Cut List For Furring Strips for 8x10 Wood and PVC A-Frame Greenhouse
- Table 4. Cut List Plastic Sheeting for 8x10 Wood and PVC A-Frame Greenhouse
- Table 5. Cut List For Door & Door Frames
- Table 6. Material List for Extended Lengths of the 8 Foot wide Wood and PVC A-Frame Greenhouse

www.ingramcontent.com/pod-product-compliance
Lightning Source LLC
Chambersburg PA
CBHW071832080526
44589CB00012B/995